GLADSTONE'S
GAMES *TO GO*

GLADSTONE'S
GAMES *TO GO*

VERBAL VOLLEYS, COIN CONTESTS, DOT DUELS, AND OTHER GAMES FOR BOREDOM-FREE DAYS →

BY JIM GLADSTONE

QUIRK BOOKS
PHILADELPHIA

Library of Congress Cataloging in Publication Number: 2003097347
ISBN: 1-931686-96-3
Printed in Singapore
Typeset in CronoMM and Helvetica

Designed and illustrated by Susan Van Horn
Edited by Erin Slonaker

Distributed in North America by Chronicle Books
85 Second Street
San Francisco, CA 94105

10 9 8 7 6 5 4 3 2

Quirk Books
215 Church Street
Philadelphia, PA 19106
www.quirkbooks.com

CONTENTS

Dear Reader,

I don't believe in boredom.

So I don't rely on boards.

Since I was a kid, playing games has been one of my favorite ways to stave off the doldrums of the occasional idle hour. On birthdays and holidays, I collected box after box of cardboard and plastic diversions, from Monopoly® and Stratego® to Mousetrap® and Ker-Plunk®. But the games that proved most engaging—and the ones I've continued to play long after my last Cootie® antenna disappeared into the nooks and crannies of a long-gone sofa—were the games that didn't require any special equipment, just a friend or two and some spare time. Games like I Went to Grandmother's House, Geography, and Ghost, which my Mom and Dad taught my brothers and me on long drives to the beach. (All three are updated and included in this book.)

Part of the reason games like these have become longstanding favorites has to do with the way my life's pace has picked up in adulthood. I'm less likely to have idle hours than idle minutes, and instead of occurring at home with a closetful of toys nearby, they hit me in sneak attacks while I'm sitting on trains, waiting for flights, or sitting in a hotel lobby. I tend not to carry a Scrabble® set with me. Sure, I've usually got a laptop and a PDA handy, but since most of my working hours are spent alone staring at pixellated text and images, computer games have never cut it for me. So now I'm the crazy guy who leans over to my traveling companions—or even to a stranger in the SkyLounge—and says "Wanna play a game with me?"

The boardless games featured in this book are terrific icebreakers, enjoyable pastimes, and—in many cases—thoroughly absorbing entertainment. The likes of Ex Post Facto, Bongo, and Meta-Boxes can be played in twenty minutes or less, but they can also lead to endless hours of strategic thinking and the invention of new variations.

It's that playful impulse to invent, imagine, and adapt that ultimately made the book so much fun to write and will hopefully add to the pleasure you take from it. Yes, every game I've included has clearly presented rules—but rules are meant to be broken, transformed, and rewritten. After fiddling with the rules of old-fashioned Grandmother's House, I came up with new-fangled Chain Reaction, which quickly became a café favorite of my word-loving friends. Bongo was born when I began musing over a way to combine Boggle® and Bingo.

When set free of pre-printed boards and boxes, games are like folksongs; they're yours to reinvent and pass along. So, please, after you try these games, spin off your own variations and hybrids. Permit your mind to go wild. Think off the board and out of the box.

Let my book be your plaything!

Yours in good fun,

Jim Gladstone

Jim@GoGladstone.com

FIVE HOT REASONS TO BE A PLAYER!

#1 | Boredom Bites!

Stow this one little book in your glove compartment, briefcase, or backpack and you'll always have more than 50 entertaining activities on hand. Whether you're sitting in a café, caught in a traffic jam, or stuck at home on a rainy Saturday, you'll find an ideal way to ditch the doldrums.

#2 | Your Tank Is Always Full

Books of puzzles, mindteasers, and wordsearches are only good for a single read-through. Once you've solved them, they're out of gas. Every game in this book can be played over and over—and differently each time.

#3 | Your Inner Child Deserves It

Indulge your sense of nostalgia by reconnecting with some of the greatest games you played as a kid. We've tweaked them so they'll present a challenge, but they'll still bring you back.

#4 | Your Brain Needs a Vacation

Dive into a world where every problem has a solution, there are clear rules for dealing with anything that happens, and everyone you play with is only in it for the fun.

#5 | And of Course . . . Cheap Thrills!

In addition to brand-new games, this book features elegant pen-and-pencil variations of Battleship®, Mastermind®, Boggle®, Scattergories®, and many more of your favorite games. Why spend more than $100 for less-portable plastic versions at a toy store?

ICON KEY

Can be played solitaire.

For exactly two players.

For two or more players.

For four or more players.

Paper and pen needed.

Paper and a different colored pen for each player needed.

Separate paper and pens for each player needed.

One coin required.

Multiple coins required.

Can be played silently.

Likely to result in outbursts of silliness.

Timer needed.

Optional equipment.

HANDS-FREE GAMING
NO EQUIPMENT WHATSOEVER!

GRANDMOTHER'S HOUSE

While driving to grandmother's house—or any other destination far enough away to provoke cries of "Are we there yet?"—parents have long depended on this classic memory game to keep small fry from going bonkers in the backseat. If cherished memories of carsickness don't inspire you to give the rather simple original game a nostalgic whirl with friends or your kids, try Gourmet Grandma, the more challenging variation on page 16.

OBJECT OF THE GAME

To memorize a string of alphabetically ordered words that gets longer each time a player takes a turn.

HOW TO PLAY

Players speak aloud, rotating through the group, each adding an item to an alphabetically stocked picnic basket of one-word foodstuffs. For example:

PLAYER 1	I went to grandmother's house, and in my picnic basket I brought an APPLE.
PLAYER 2	. . . I brought an APPLE and a BANANA.
PLAYER 3	. . . an APPLE, a BANANA, and a COOKIE.
PLAYER 4	. . . an APPLE, a BANANA, a COOKIE, and a DOUGHNUT.
PLAYER 1	. . . an APPLE, a BANANA, a COOKIE, a DOUGHNUT, and an EGG.

HOW TO WIN

Players are eliminated when they suffer a memory lapse. On the next turn in the game above, for instance, if Player 2 can't remember what **C** stands for (or says "**CHICKEN**" or "**CAKE**" by mistake), Player 3 gets a chance to recite the chain from the beginning. If Player 3 succeeds, Player 2 is eliminated and the others continue the game. If Player 3 *also* fails, Player 4 has the opportunity to eliminate both Player 2 *and* Player 3 by successfully reciting the full chain and adding his **F** word at the end.

The last remaining player is the winner.

NOTES & NIT-PICKS

→ The author wishes to receive neither recipes nor complaints of chipped teeth, but for this game alone, **XYLOPHONE**s and **X-RAY**s are officially declared edible. (Even the magisterial *Oxford Companion to Food* has not a single entry under **X**.) In general, some flexibility is always suggested, especially when children and adults are playing together. It's swell that Dad knows about the Japanese noodles called **UDON** but consider letting little Suzy sneak an **UMBRELLA** in the basket. (It would come in handy in case of rain, after all.)

→ If you make it all the way to **ZUCCHINI**, the chain loops back around to **A**. Players must always repeat the *full* list on their turns, from the first **APPLE** all the way into the second alphabet:

... an **APPLE**, a **BANANA**, a **COOKIE** ... a **XYLOPHONE**, a **YAM**, a **ZUCCHINI**, an **AVOCADO**, and a **BEET.**

→ Because the rhythm of spoken words can be an aid to memory, players must always repeat the chain as a sentence rather than a straight list:

"... **FLOUR**, a **GRAPEFRUIT**, and a **HAMBURGER**," not simply

"... **FLOUR**, **GRAPEFRUIT**, **HAMBURGER**."

GOURMET GRANDMA

After a few rounds of Grandmother's House (see page 14), sticking to an alphabetical list of items tends to get repetitive. If you're playing with a group of adults or older kids, try cranking things up a notch by reciting the list without articles or conjunctions and using the last letter of each item as the first letter of the following item. The more sophisticated the palates of the players, the more fun the game gets.

OBJECT OF THE GAME

To memorize a string of words that gets longer each time a player takes a turn.

HOW TO PLAY

In the same style as Grandmother's House, players speak aloud, rotating through the group, each adding an item to a list of items placed in an imaginary picnic basket. This time, though, the last letter of the preceding word is the first letter of the next. For example:

PLAYER 1	APPLE
PLAYER 2	APPLE, EGGPLANT
PLAYER 3	APPLE, EGGPLANT, TIRAMISU (Italian rum-soaked pastry!)
PLAYER 4	APPLE, EGGPLANT, TIRAMISU, UNI (sea urchin sushi!)
PLAYER 1	APPLE, EGGPLANT, TIRAMISU, UNI, INJERA (Ethiopian crepes!)

NOTES & NIT-PICKS

Players can come to a consensus on each item as it's played, but here are some basic guidelines for choosing acceptable ingredients:

→ All items should be edible.

→ Two-word items are allowed: **ICE CREAM, PORK CHOP, LIMA BEAN.**

→ No unneccessary category names: **MOZZARELLA** and **CHEDDAR,** not **MOZZARELLA CHEESE** and **CHEDDAR CHEESE; BLUE CHEESE** and **AMERICAN CHEESE** would be fine.

→ No brand names: **PEANUT BUTTER,** not **SKIPPY.**

→ No unnecessary plurals: **TOMATO,** not **TOMATOES; GRAPES** or **CHERRIES** would be fine because they generally come in bunches.

→ No flavor repeats: No **GRAPE JELLY** if **GRAPE JUICE** or **GRAPES** has been played.

→ No product repeats: No **PEACH JELLY** if **GRAPE JELLY** has been played.

There will always be debatable items (**IODIZED SALT? GREEN APPLE? INSTANT COFFEE? FRENCH BREAD?**). Just be sure to conduct your debates quickly—*you've got to keep the whole list memorized while you mull over the latest addition!* Play should pause if anyone becomes nauseated imagining a Dagwood sandwich made from all the ingredients in the list.

VARIATIONS

In Gourmet Grandma, food gives the memory something to really sink its teeth into. Players can visualize the list as one enormous smorgasbord, and recollections of tastes, smells, and textures may also help them maintain longer sequences in their heads. Nonetheless, you can invent similar games around other general categories:

Geography

MISSISSIPPI, INDIA, ATLANTIC OCEAN, NEW YORK, KALAMAZOO, OKLAHOMA, ALBANIA . . .

Celebrities

BILL CLINTON, NOEL COWARD, DAVID LETTERMAN, NAOMI CAMPBELL, LANCE ARMSTRONG . . .

Zoology

AARDVARK, KANGAROO, OPOSSUM, MACAW, WOMBAT, TOUCAN, NEWT, TAPIR . . .

GHOST

 Fragments of words float through the air and go through shapeshifting transformations in this classic play-out-loud game. Try not to get spooked when things begin to move in unexpected directions; the key to winning at Ghost is to accept surprises and approach them with an open mind. Completely hands-free, Ghost is great for car-trips—but feel free to play in any of your favorite haunts.

OBJECT OF THE GAME

To *avoid* spelling words of three or more letters.

HOW TO PLAY

A round begins with Player 1 announcing any letter of the alphabet. Player 2 then repeats Player 1's letter, adding another letter.

PLAYER 1	A
PLAYER 2	A-G

Player 3 (or Player 1, in a two-person game) must add a letter to the chain *without completing a word.*

PLAYER 3	A-G-I

Had he added E or O, Player 3 would have lost the round because **AGE** and **AGO** are complete words.

Play continues to the next player. From here on, the player on each subsequent turn has two choices. He or she can either add to the chain without completing a word, or *challenge* the previous player to complete the current chain.

PLAYER 3	A-G-I
PLAYER 4	I challenge you. I don't think you know a word that begins A-G-I.

A challenged player must respond with a viable word *immediately*. It is each player's responsibility to have a word in mind when adding a letter to the chain.

PLAYER 3	AGILE!

Because the challenge was successfully met by Player 3, Player 4 loses the round. (Had Player 3 failed to meet the challenge, Player 3 would have lost the round.)

STRATEGY TIP: BLUFFING

Here's the situation: It's your turn, but you can't think of a way to avoid completing a word or to extend the chain toward a longer word, but you suspect the prior player will be able to respond to a challenge. You still have an option:

Don't reveal your inner despair. Keep a poker face and calmly add a letter to the chain. You're bluffing. It's possible that the next player will challenge you and you'll lose the round, but it's also possible that your apparent confidence will lead the next player to bluff as well, in which case responsibility to meet a challenge is shifted to him.

There's something else that can happen if you bluff, particularly during the early turns of a round: Sometimes the next player is able to come up with a word that you overlooked, and your bluff letter becomes a legitimate link in the chain.

Here's a four-player sample round, with a look at the strategy behind each player's moves:

	CALLED LETTERS	THOUGHT PROCESS
PLAYER 1	A	A is for ANTIDISESTABLISH-MENTARIANISM
PLAYER 2	A-G	I'm thinking of AGAPE.
PLAYER 3	A-G-I	I'm thinking of AGILE.

→

PLAYER 4	A-G-I-T	I'm clueless! But I'll bluff with the letter T—it's common enough.
PLAYER 1	(pause) A-G-I-T-A	I'm delaying because I can't think of anything. Oh wait! I've got it: AGITATE.
PLAYER 2	Bzzzzzzzt! You lose! AGITA is a complete word.	AGITA means acid indigestion.

Here's a way this round could have gone on a bit longer:

	CALLED LETTERS	THOUGHT PROCESS
PLAYER 1	A-G-I-T-P	I've got one! AGITPROP, which means political propaganda.
PLAYER 2	I chall—Wait! A-G-I-T-P-R	A-G-I-T-P!? She must be bluffing. Wait! I see it: AGITPROP.
PLAYER 3	A-G-I-T-P-R-O	AGITPROP is the only word I can think of.
PLAYER 4	Urgh! I lose! A-G-I-T-P-R-O-P	There's no point in challenging. Everyone's thinking AGITPROP, there's no way I can avoid it.

SCORING

There are two options for scoring, depending on how much time you want to spend playing. (Time estimates below are based on four-player games.) The fewer the players, the briefer the playing time.

Long Game (Approximately 45 minutes)

Each time a player loses a round, he is given one letter of the word **GHOST.** Players are eliminated when they lose five rounds (**G-H-O-S-T**). Last person standing wins.

A long game can be divided over several sessions. You only have to keep track of how many **GHOST** letters each player has accumulated.

Short Game (Approximately 10 minutes)

When a player loses a round, he or she is eliminated. Each subsequent round includes one less player. Last person left after all the eliminations is the winner.

●

SUPERGHOST

 If the basic game of Ghost (see page 18) has grown too simple for you and your friends, add a twist and the game becomes challenging all over again.

HOW TO PLAY

Review the rules for Ghost on page 18. Superghost follows these same rules with one major exception: On each turn, a player may add to either the beginning *or* the end of the letter chain. For example:

	CALLED LETTERS	THOUGHT PROCESS
PLAYER 1	P	PEACE
PLAYER 2	I-P	SHIP
PLAYER 3	I-P-L	DIPLOMA

or

	CALLED LETTERS	THOUGHT PROCESS
PLAYER 1	P	HAPLESS
PLAYER 2	I-P	SHIP
PLAYER 3	C-I-P	INCIPIENT

If you enjoy Superghost, try Wordcore (see page 29).

SCORING

Follow the same scoring as for Ghost.

POLTERGEIST

 This one's for hardcore game nuts only! A poltergeist is a rowdy spirit that rearranges furniture and otherwise shoves things around. In tribute to that most reckless of ghosts, this game uses all the rules of Superghost (see page 21) and also permits players to insert new letters *within* existing chains.

HOW TO PLAY

Letters are called out just as for Superghost, but letters can now be inserted *between* existing letters, not just added to the beginning or the end. The *order* of letters in the chain may not be changed, however.

	CALLED LETTERS	THOUGHT PROCESS
PLAYER 1	T	TOWER
PLAYER 2	T-A	TALK
PLAYER 3	T-R-A	TRANCE

Player 3 could have played a letter in a number of different positions. See, for example:

	CALLED LETTERS	THOUGHT PROCESS
PLAYER 3	T-H-A	THAN
	T-A-L	TALON
	R-T-A	CURTAIN

Things get complicated quickly!

SCORING

Follow the same scoring as for Ghost (see page 20).

NOTE

Poltergeist is too tough for small kids, but the skills needed to play can be taught with License to Spell (see page 28), another no-equipment game that's ideal for car trips.

CHAIN REACTION

 Here's a word game that, on its surface, seems quite simple. Simply make chains of linking words—how hard is that? But once you get tangled up in a long chain, you'll see that there's more to this game than meets the eye. Chain Reaction introduces a whole new level of complexity—and hilarity—as words and phrases morph and mate in unexpected ways.

OBJECT OF THE GAME

To form a string of compound words or two-word phrases. There are strategies to win the game, but sometimes attempting to make the longest string possible is plenty of fun in itself!

HOW TO PLAY

The game begins with Player 1 announcing a compound word or a common two-word phrase.

On each succeeding turn, players repeat the existing chain of words and add a final word that forms a new compound word, a two-syllable word, or common short expression when paired with the previous end word. For example:

PLAYER 1	POST OFFICE
PLAYER 2	POST OFFICE PARTY
PLAYER 3	POST OFFICE PARTY ANIMAL
PLAYER 1	POST OFFICE PARTY ANIMAL CRACKER
PLAYER 2	POST OFFICE PARTY ANIMAL CRACKER BARREL
PLAYER 3	POST OFFICE PARTY ANIMAL CRACKER BARREL CHEST
PLAYER 1	POST OFFICE PARTY ANIMAL CRACKER BARREL CHEST NUT
PLAYER 2	POST OFFICE PARTY ANIMAL CRACKER BARREL CHEST NUT BUTTER
PLAYER 3	POST OFFICE PARTY ANIMAL CRACKER BARREL CHEST NUT BUTTER CUP
PLAYER 1	POST OFFICE PARTY ANIMAL CRACKER BARREL CHEST NUT BUTTER CUP FULL

→

HOW TO WIN

There are three ways to win:

Memory Lapse

In a two-player game, if one person can't recall the chain, his or her oppo-nent automatically wins. In a multi-player game, if a player can't properly repeat the chain aloud, she falls out of the game and play continues until all players but one have been eliminated.

Challenge

Sometimes the last compound word creates a link that is difficult to built on. In these cases, the player who is up next can pose a challenge to the previous player. For example, if Player 2 says "**COW BOY FRIEND SHIP SHAPE SHIFT WORK PLACE MAT,**" and Player 3 cannot think of a way to build on **MAT,** she can challenge Player 2 to do it.

If Player 2 comes up with a workable word, Player 3 is eliminated. If not, Player 2 is eliminated and the chain is continued, with Player 3 build-ing from **PLACE**.

If there are only two players, the winner of a challenge automatically wins the game.

Looping

If a player successfully builds the chain by adding the exact same word that began the game, he or she automatically wins.

PLAYER 1	WORK PLACE
PLAYER 2	WORK PLACE CARD
PLAYER 3	WORK PLACE CARD CARRYING
PLAYER 1	WORK PLACE CARD CARRYING CASE
PLAYER 2	WORK PLACE CARD CARRYING CASE WORK *I looped it!*

NOTES

Because the game is played aloud, homonyms may be used inter-changeably: Spelling doesn't matter, only the sound of the words.

Taking advantage of homonyms can increase your flexibility. (It also makes for more entertaining chains.)

HASH BROWN BEAR

can become

HASH BROWN BEAR CUB   *or*   **HASH BROWN BARE NAKED**

Unlike most word games, which disallow proper nouns, Chain Reaction is more fun—and lasts longer—when brand names and common terms that include names are permitted. Players can come to a consensus on the eligibility of each word or phrase as it's played; it's a good idea to be permissive with brand names such as Pop Tart and ViewMaster. Likewise, consider accepting first names in contexts such as "**HILL BILLY GOAT CHEESE**" and "**LONG JOHN DOE NUT.**"

CIRCUS TENT POLE LOCK SMITH BROTHERS KARAMAZOV—*OOPS!*

HINKY PINKY

Warning: This is the game most likely to induce groans. Hinky Pinky encourages the sort of goofy, juvenile wordplay that made you want to hide under the kitchen table when dear old Dad started his suppertime comedy routines. So, remember, it's a sign of maturity and acceptance to play this one.

OBJECT OF THE GAME

To guess the answers to rhyming riddles created by other players. You could certainly figure out a way to keep score and crown a winner, but that would be as silly as the game itself.

HOW TO PLAY

The game begins—often spontaneously—with somebody crying out "Hinky Pinky!" He then presents a clue that suggests a rhyming phrase consisting of two two-syllable words.

Anyone in the group who can figure out the clue responds by calling out the rhyming words. The guesser may then present a clue to another word pair. The game continues ad infinitum—or ad nauseum, as the case may be!

"HINK PINK" indicates the answer will be two one-syllable words.

"HINKY PINKY" indicates the answer will be two two-syllable words.

"HINKETY PINKETY" indicates the answer will be two three-syllable words.

HINKY PINKY!	It's a war among cows!	A cattle battle!
HINK PINK!	It's a ball of noise!	A round sound!
HINK PINK!	It's a bird in the sand.	A dune loon!
HINKETY PINKETY!	It's an energy source that's full of praise!"	A flattery battery!
HINKY PINKY!	It's a cross between a pet fish and a pet dog!	A guppy puppy!
HINK PINK!	It's what we're playing!	A lame game!

Actually, with the right crowd, Hinky Pinky can be loads of fun. It can also be tailored to be appropriate for any audience, from college students inclined to double entendre to toddlers who are more nursery rhyme oriented.

HINKY PINKY PUZZLERS

Can you guess the answers to these sample riddles?

HINK PINK	HINKY PINKY	HINKETY PINKETY
A purple gorilla	A Vidalia callus	Island nightwear
A celebrity buggy	A jaundiced greeting	An artistic getaway
Pink stockings	A flow of innards	A frozen Schwinn

Answers on page 144.

LICENSE TO SPELL

Though less than a rigorous challenge for most grown-up game enthusiasts, License to Spell is an amusing way to pass the time on car trips. It's also a simple and entertaining method to begin teaching kids the skills that will prepare them for the likes of Ghost (see page 18), Wordcore (see page 29), and other complex spelling games. License to Spell can be played while on a road trip or anyplace from which the players can observe passing vehicles. Players should be seated so they are facing the same direction.

OBJECT OF THE GAME

To identify words using the groups of letters found on license plates.

HOW TO PLAY

As traffic passes by, players take note of license plates. Vanity plates are ignored. When a player sees a plate that includes three or more letters, she points to it and calls out a word that includes the plate's letters, preceded by an identifying remark about the vehicle. For example:

A player spotting a red Ford Mustang with the Pennsylvania license plate **DWR•386** might call "**MUSTANG! DRAWER!**" Other acceptable calls for this same car would be "**RED! WIDOWER!**" or "**PENNSYLVANIA! DOWRY!**"

To be acceptable, called words must include *all* of the letters in the plate, in the order they appear. Once any player calls an acceptable word for a plate, the plate cannot be revisited.

HOW TO WIN

License to Spell is fun to play without keeping score, as players jostle to generate words more quickly than their opponents. However, you can score one point for a player each time she calls an acceptable word.

In heavy traffic, it's possible that opponents won't always notice the same cars, in which case you may want to designate one non-competing passenger as a neutral judge to confirm spottings.

WORDCORE

 Wordcore is derived from a game called MischMasch, originally popularized in the late nineteenth century by *Alice in
Wonderland* author Lewis Carroll, who also created Doublets
(see page 101). It can be seen as a cousin of Ghost (see page 18),
although Wordcore encourages more mischievous bluffing.

OBJECT OF THE GAME

To come up with words that contain specific sequences of letters.

HOW TO PLAY

Player 1 announces a core of two or more letters; for example, **GHL**.

Player 2 has two minutes in which to respond in one of three ways:

→ He can name a word that includes the core: **HIGHLIGHT.**

→ He can pose a challenge: "I don't believe there's a word with that core."

→ He can withdraw from the round.

Player 2 then receives a score for the round:

→ If Player 2 correctly names a word containing the core, he gets
1 point.

→ If Player 2 poses a challenge and Player 1 has been bluffing and
cannot immediately name a word containing the core, Player 2
scores 2 points.

→ If Player 2 poses a challenge and Player 1 can immediately name a
word containing the core, Player 2 loses 2 points.

→ If Player 2 withdraws, he automatically loses 1 point.

Next, Player 2 gives Player 1 a core of letters, and the process is repeated.

NOTE

A core can be located at the beginning or end of a word, not just in the middle. For example:

PNE	PNEUMONIA
DZE	ADZE (A two-bladed axe!)

HOW TO WIN

The first player to score 10 points is the winner. If Player 2 reaches 10 before Player 1, he is obligated to provide one more core, giving Player 1 a last chance to win or tie the game.

SIX DEGREES

Inspired by the 1993 movie version of the award-winning John Guare play *Six Degrees of Separation*, three students at Pennsylvania's Albright College—Craig Fass, Mike Ginelli, and Brian Turtle—came up with the nifty movie trivia game they called "Six Degrees of Kevin Bacon." The game exploded in popularity when comedian Jon Stewart featured it on his MTV program. Kevin Bacon may now be more famous for his role in this game than for any of his acting gigs. Try linking other movie stars, too—you don't have to limit yourself to just Kevin Bacon.

OBJECT OF THE GAME

To link two movie stars through a chain of overlapping co-stars.

HOW TO PLAY

Player 1 names two celebrities: **WILL SMITH** and **KEVIN BACON**.

Player 2 links them in as few steps as possible:

> **WILL SMITH** was in *Six Degrees of Separation* with
>> **STOCKARD CHANNING;**
>
> **STOCKARD CHANNING** was in *To Wong Foo . . .* with
>> **WESLEY SNIPES;**
>
> **WESLEY SNIPES** was in *Collateral Damage* with
>> **ARNOLD SCHWARZENEGGER;**
>
> **ARNOLD SCHWARZENEGGER** was in *True Lies* with
>> **JAMIE LEE CURTIS;**
>
> **JAMIE LEE CURTIS** was in *Queens Logic* with
>> **KEVIN BACON.**

That's five degrees!

→

Play continues clockwise around the group, with each player trying to make the connection in fewer links. For example:

> **WILL SMITH** was in *The Legend of Bagger Vance* with
>> **CHARLIZE THERON;**
> **CHARLIZE THERON** was in *Trapped* with
>> **KEVIN BACON.**

Just two degrees!

HOW TO WIN

The goal is to get the *least* number of points. Players score one point for each degree they use to connect the celebrities. If a player gives up, she scores 10 points. If *all* players give up, the proposer has three minutes to demonstrate that a chain is possible. If the proposer cannot come up with a workable chain, she scores 10 points and the other players each get 10 points deducted from their tallies.

VARIATION

For the gossip-column addicted, connections can be expanded to include not just overlaps in film roles, but romantic entanglements as well.

Here's one possible route from Batman to Robin, **MICHAEL KEATON** to **CHRIS O'DONNELL:**

> **MICHAEL KEATON** was in *Mr. Mom* with
>> **TERI GARR;**
> **TERI GARR** was in *The Conversation* with
>> **HARRISON FORD;**
> **HARRISON FORD** has been dating **CALISTA FLOCKHART** for years;
> **CALISTA FLOCKHART** was on *Ally McBeal* with
>> **LUCY LIU;**
> **LUCY LIU** was in *Charlie's Angels* with
>> **DREW BARRYMORE;**
> **DREW BARRYMORE** was in *Mad Love* with
>> **CHRIS O'DONNELL.**

Five degrees!

○

STAR QUALITIES

If you excel at Six Degrees (see page 31), this one will thrill you to no end. A people-watching game, Star Qualities is essentially non-competitive. It's a great way to kill time while waiting in lines at airports, theme parks, and other crowded places.

SETUP

Players should situate themselves so that they are facing the same direction and looking at a crowd or a stream of pedestrians. Sitting outdoors at a busy café and in the lobby of a bustling hotel are ideal play situations.

OBJECT OF THE GAME

To identify passersby by their minor resemblances to famous people.

HOW TO PLAY

Players scan the crowd. When one player notices someone who resembles a celebrity, he whispers the celebrity's name and a "likeness percentage."

For example, when spotting a dead ringer for the famous country singer, Player 1 says, "**95% DOLLY PARTON.**"

The other players then try to identify whom Player 1 is referring to.

The game becomes more challenging when the likenesses are lesser, and when the "stars" are less famous and less unique-looking. Well-versed movie geeks will *combine* these elements to come up with challenges like "**20% STEVE BUSCEMI**" or "**30% VIVIAN VANCE.**"

HOW TO LOSE

Get caught gawking (or worse, pointing!) at a stranger and giggling.

VARIATION

Constellation Qualities

Combine more than one celebrity resemblance in your descriptions. For example, if you spot a short, chubby man in a sequined smoking jacket, you might say "**40% DANNY DEVITO and 10% CHER.**"

CHANGE IS GOOD!
COIN GAMES

MOLECULAR FLIP

Here's a game that tests your ability to solve spatial logic problems. It's great for solo play, but the extra pressure of playing with a group will appeal to highly competitive gamers as they race to see who can solve the problems first. Note-taking is absolutely forbidden during play.

SETUP

Set out nine coins so you have a random mix of heads and tails. Place the coins in a 3 x 3 formation in the center of a table or other flat surface. This is now your Target Square.

Set out nine more coins and arrange them randomly into another 3 x 3 square. This is your Flipping Square. (It should have a different arrangement of heads and tails than the Target Square. If it happens to be the same, flip the coins again to generate a different pattern.)

Target Square   *Flipping Square*

Each player should create the same Flipping Square, with heads and tails in the exact same positions.

OBJECT OF THE GAME

To be the first player to rearrange the coins in his or her Flipping Square so that it exactly matches the arrangement of the Target Square.

HOW TO PLAY

The board is composed of several "molecules," or groupings of coins.

Players flip molecules in order to arrive at the head-and-tails pattern set out in the Target Square.

The Molecular Laws

Corner Molecules

These are the four coins grouped together in the corners of the grid; there are four Corner Molecules. One Corner Molecule is indicated below.

T-Molecules

These molecules are clustered not in squares but in Ts. The four T-Molecules are:

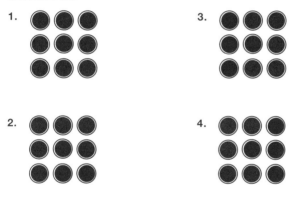

Cross Molecule

Branching out from the center position is a cross; this forms the Cross Molecule. There is, naturally, only one Cross Molecule in the grid.

Play goes around the table like this: Player 1 chooses a molecule to flip over. Next, Player 2 chooses a molecule to flip over on her grid. She can choose to mimic Player 1's move or to flip a different molecule entirely.

→

Each player makes one move in succession on his or her own grid. Play continues clockwise around the table until one player gets his Flipping Square arranged exactly like the Target Square, winning the game.

When one player achieves a match, anyone who has had one turn less than the matching player may go again in an attempt to tie for first place.

With more than two players, the game can continue in a competition for second place, third place, and so on.

Sample Transformation

Target Square

Flipping Square

First Flip: Right T-Molecule

Second Flip: Upper T-Molecule

Third Flip: Lower Left Corner Molecule

> Patience is a virtue.
> Don't give up! Using the molecular laws, *any* 3 x 3 arrangement of heads and tails can be transformed into any other.

Fourth Flip: Cross Molecule

CLUSTER BUSTER

Divide and conquer is clearly the key strategy for this game, but the more players you've got—and the more objects you play with—the more challenging you'll find it. The setup of Cluster Buster can be as much fun as the play itself if you move beyond coins and use a colorful variety of playing pieces: You begin by creating a crazy mosaic, then erase it as the game goes on!

SETUP

Arrange any number of coins or other small objects in any number of clusters on a tabletop. To ensure fairness, each player can simultaneously arrange some of the objects. Objects in a cluster must touch at least one other object in that cluster. Clusters composed of only one object are fine.

OBJECT OF THE GAME

To avoid removing the final object.

HOW TO PLAY

Player 1 removes one or two coins from the table.

→ Any one coin can be removed, whether it is standing alone or is part of a larger cluster.

→ If a pair is selected, the two coins must be touching each other within the cluster.

Play continues in turn, with each player removing one or two coins according to the conditions above.

→

HOW TO WIN

In a two-player game, the player forced to remove the final coin loses. When more than two people are playing, the player who removes the final coin is eliminated, a new arrangement of clusters is set up, and play begins again without the eliminated player. The process is repeated until all players but one are eliminated.

VARIATIONS

The game can be customized to suit a variety of settings:

→ Use clusters of sticks or stones on a camping trip.

→ Play with seashells on the beach.

→ Use candies or chips instead of coins so players can snack as they remove pieces.

→ Play with unbagged groceries on your kitchen table; whenever someone removes an item, she can put it away in its proper cupboard.

FLIP STRIP

See how long it takes you to figure out a winning system for this game. It's underpinned by some relatively simple math that can let you hustle your opponents if you know it! Who knows if your opponent has already cracked the code! (For more on the mathematical secrets of games, see Nim on page 62.)

SETUP

Flip 15 coins, one at a time. Line them on the tabletop as they land. The goal is to have a random mix of heads and tails.

(If you don't have enough coins, tear up 15 bits of paper, flip one coin, and mark each bit of paper heads or tails.)

OBJECT OF THE GAME

To turn every coin in the row heads up.

HOW TO PLAY

Players alternate moves. On each move, a player must turn over either one or two coins. Coin turns are governed by these conditions:

→ If one coin is turned, it must be turned from tails to heads.

→ If two coins are turned, the coin farther to the right must be turned from tails to heads, but the other coin may be turned either way.

→

Four Legal Moves (Red coins are about to be turned)

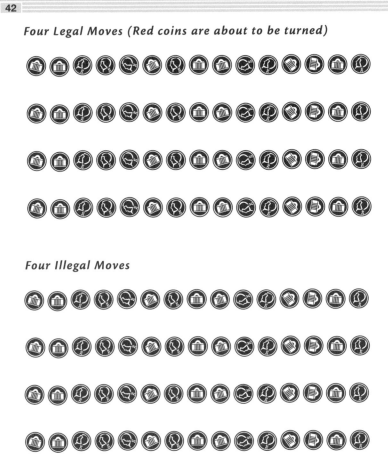

Four Illegal Moves

HOW TO WIN

The player who makes a move leaving all coins heads up is the winner.

VARIATION
On the Flip Side

Try playing the exact same game, but with the opposite goal: The player who makes a move leaving all coins heads up is the loser.

SLIDERS

Part of the appeal of Sliders is the strange sense of ritual at the beginning of the game. Secret numbers are scrawled, then revealed, and finally, a miniature landscape of towers is constructed. If you play in public, casual observers will first be mystified, then be drawn to you. Be prepared to let others in on the fun!

SETUP

Draw a strip of eight or more boxes on a piece of paper. Mark the boxes in alphabetical order, except for the last box, which should be marked **HOME:**

A	B	C	D	E	F	G	H	HOME

OBJECT OF THE GAME

To be the player to move the final piece into **HOME.**

HOW TO PLAY

Each player secretly writes down a number between 0 and 3 for each of the lettered boxes.

The players reveal their numbers and add them together to determine a total (between 0 and 6) for each box. That many coins (or sugar cubes, matchsticks, or other tokens) are piled on each box.

Each player secretly writes down an additional number between 1 and 3. These numbers are revealed and added to determine the Maximum Slide.

Player 1 now slides any one coin from any box toward home. The coin can be slid any number of boxes, up to the Maximum Slide. If the Maximum Slide is 3, a coin in Box B could be slid to box C, D, or E.

Player 2 now slides any one coin according to the same rule, and play alternates until the last coin is placed in Home.

HOW TO WIN

The player to move the final piece into **HOME** is the winner.

TARGET TRACER

Compared with the rest of the games in this book, Target Tracer is for jocks. It actually requires a teensy bit of hand-eye coordination! Play a few rounds and you'll be transported back to the tabletops of your elementary school cafeteria.

SETUP

Trace the circumference of a coin at the center of a large piece of paper. Set the paper on a large, flat surface. This is the target.

OBJECT OF THE GAME

To slide, spin, or flip a coin so that it lands within a marked target.

HOW TO PLAY

Player 1 positions the coin anywhere within the edge of the paper and attempts to launch it into the target using only one of the following techniques. Before play begins, players agree which coin-moving technique will be used for the game.

Surface Slide

With your fingertip, push and release the coin so that it slides along the surface of the table.

Face Flick

Stand the coin on its edge using your index finger. With the index finger of your other hand, quickly flick the face of the coin so that it spins and moves forward.

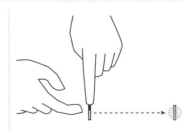

Edge Flick

Stand the coin on its edge using your index finger. With the index finger of your other hand, quickly flick the edge of the coin so that it propels forward.

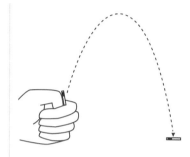

Air Flip

Make a fist with one hand. Turn your wrist so that your thumb is up. Rest the coin on your thumb, then flick your thumb up, launching the coin forward through the air.

Wherever the coin lands, its circumference is traced, making an additional target. As the game progresses, some traced circles will overlap. As circles overlap, their outermost perimeters are considered merged, forming larger targets.

HOW TO WIN

The first player to land a coin completely within a target without overlapping an outer perimeter wins.

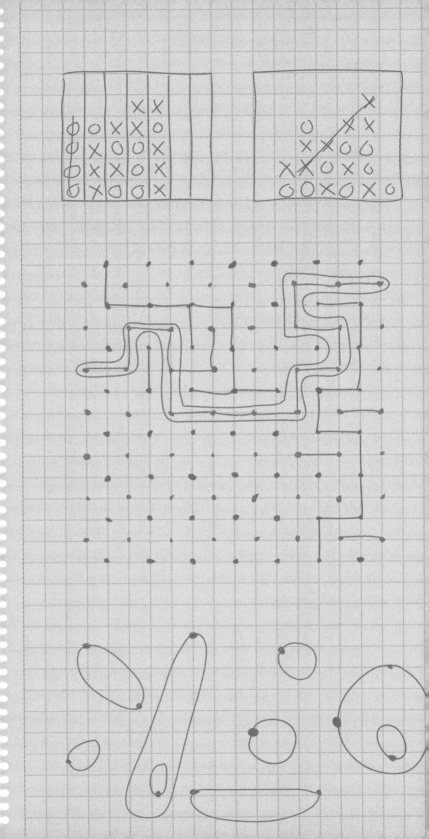

THE PEN IS MIGHTIER THAN THE BOARD
PEN-AND-PAPER GAMES

BIG-TAC-TOE

You've got to draw the line somewhere. We're drawing it at Tic-Tac-Toe, the lobotomized seventh-generation descendant of the classic Japanese strategy game Go.

You already know how to play, you know how to fix a win, and you realize that without Whoopi Goldberg or Paul Lynde in the center square, it's a real snooze. Instead, try this simple twist. The more players—and the larger your grid—the more challenging the game becomes.

OBJECT OF THE GAME

To form a string of four of your marks, horizontally, vertically, or diagonally.

SETUP

Draw a grid of 10 x 10 squares (or larger). Determine a letter to be used as a mark by each player (**S, T, Z, V,** etc.).

HOW TO PLAY

Player 1 makes his mark in any space on the grid. Other players follow in turn.

HOW TO WIN

Line up four of your mark in a string.

VARIATIONS

→ The larger your grid, the more reasonable it is to play complex variations. Try playing with four people on a full sheet of graph paper.

→ Require longer strings, e.g., "Six in a row wins."

→ Require more strings, e.g., "Two strings of four in a row wins." When playing this variation, players must agree in advance whether strings are allowed to share a mark—for example, does the position below count as a win for **V?**

3-D TIC-TAC-TOE

You've got to line up four of your marks across three dimensions in this simple but more challenging version of Old Snoozy. The key is not to let your attention get fixed on any single level of the quadruple-decker playing field.

SETUP

Draw this diagram on a piece of paper.

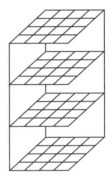

OBJECT OF THE GAME

Line up four of your marks in a string. Winning strings can be completely on one level or can have one mark on each of the four planes.

HOW TO PLAY

Player 1 makes an **X** in any space on the diagram. Player 2 makes an **O** in any space on the diagram. Play alternates until someone wins by placing four marks in a row.

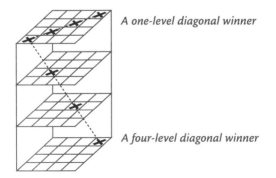

A one-level diagonal winner

A four-level diagonal winner

TAPATAN

Tic-Tac-Toe's Filipino cousin is traditionally played with beans or stones on a patterned wooden board, but it's easily adapted to require no special equipment. Tapatan offers a bit more challenge than its stateside relative because there's less gridlock. Each player only has three marks on the board at any one time. The game is fun for kids, but sharp adults will quickly realize that, just as in Tic-Tac-Toe, there are sure-fire winning strategies.

SETUP

Draw this figure on a piece of paper:

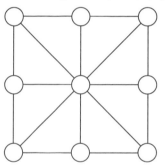

Give each player a set of three matched tokens. Six coins—three heads-up, three tails-up—are fine. Or tear small bits of paper and mark three with each player's initials.

OBJECT OF THE GAME

To get all of your tokens lined up in a row horizontally, vertically, or diagonally.

HOW TO PLAY

The game is divided into two periods: placing and moving.

→

Placing

Player 1 sets one of his tokens on any of the empty circles in the diagram. Player 2 does the same.

Placement alternates in this fashion until all six tokens have been placed.

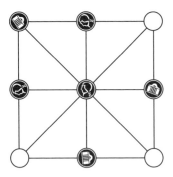

Moving

Player 1 now slides any one of his tokens to the next *unoccupied* circle along a line. Player 2 does the same. Each player must follow these rules:

- → Two tokens may never occupy the same circle.
- → Tokens may not jump an occupied circle to reach an unnoccupied circle.

Play alternates in this fashion until one player wins by lining up three tokens in a row.

BE AN INTERNATIONAL PLAYER!

Some say that love is the international language. Others say love is a game. So, perhaps games are the international language . . .

The same diagram used to play Tapatan in the Phillipines is used for similar games around the globe. Its been found carved into stones dating back as far as the Roman Empire. Here's how to play variations popular in other parts of the world:

MARELLE

During the placing period of this French variation, neither player can set his first token in the center spot.

ACHI

In Ghana, during the placing period, each player begins by setting *four* tokens on the diagram, but the goal is still to get three in a row.

PICARIA

Popular in the southwestern United States, it's believed that this game—played by the same rules as Tapatan, but with a different board configuration—originated in Spain and came to the New World with the conquistadors.

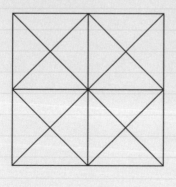

THE CAPTAIN'S MISTRESS

The Mother of All Travel Games, The Captain's Mistress got its name after Captain James Cook spent hundreds of hours playing a three-dimensional version of this game made of sculpted wood. His long years at sea left plenty of down time for playing games with his crew. The Captain's Mistress has never lost its appeal—in fact, Milton Bradley introduced a plastic version in the 1970s, calling it Connect Four. But it's even easier to play The Captain's Mistress with only pen and paper.

SETUP

Draw a grid of six rows by seven columns, called a Gravity Grid.

OBJECT OF THE GAME

To form a line of four **X**s or **O**s horizontally, vertically, or diagonally.

HOW TO PLAY

Imagine that the grid is ruled by the law of gravity. Think of the columns as chutes, and think of the **X** and **O** marks you make as marbles dropped down the chutes. On each move, a player may "drop" a mark only into the lowermost empty square of a column. (A maximum of six marks can fill a column.)

Player 1 drops an **X** into the column of her choice.

Player 2 drops an **O** into the column of her choice.

Moves alternate until one player completes a winning line of four marks in a row. Here's a series of moves from a sample game:

FIRST MOVE

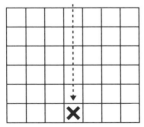

SECOND MOVE

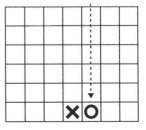

THIRD MOVE

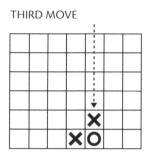

TWELFTH MOVE

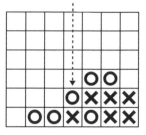

O blocks X from winning horizontally.

THIRTEENTH MOVE

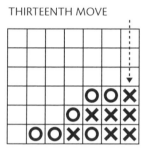

FOURTEENTH MOVE

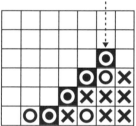

O wins on the diagonal!

VARIATIONS

→ To make the basic game last longer, play on a grid with more rows and columns.

→ More than two people can play if you use a much larger grid: Try 12 rows by 14 columns for three players or 18 rows by 21 columns for four players. Assign new players different symbols: ***, #,** or their initials. Note: The more players, the more likely that games will end in a stalemate.

MOKA

Moka was invented by Jay Laird and Mark Rosenstein in a series of brainstorming sessions during the late 1990s. The two would play at their favorite Boston and Cambridge cafés, including the late, lamented beanery that lent the game its name. Though Moka can be played anywhere with coins or pen and paper, there's a certain charming resourcefulness to using sugar packets for markers if you happen to be playing in your own favorite coffee shop.

SETUP

Each player gathers a unique set of eight similarly sized markers that have two visually distinct sides. Some handy examples:

→ 8 pennies for Player 1 and 8 dimes for Player 2

→ 8 white sugar packets for Player 1 and 8 pink artificial sweetener packets for Player 2

→ 8 matchbooks from one restaurant for Player 1 and 8 from another for Player 2

(Or, you can tear eight squares of paper and mark them with an X on one side and an O on the other, using different colored pens to make it clear whose pieces are whose.)

→ Four more objects similar in size to the playing pieces (nickels, blue sweetener packets, blank scraps of paper) are used as anchors to help delineate the playing field. They may never be moved during the game. In the following example, the anchors are coins.

Place the markers on a tabletop in the following formation:

OBJECT OF THE GAME

To create a horizontal, vertical, or diagonal line of three of your playing pieces, all with same side up.

HOW TO PLAY

Moka is played on a virtual board. Imagine that, in the setup, the markers and anchors form the perimeter of a 6 x 6 box of squares situated on a larger grid.

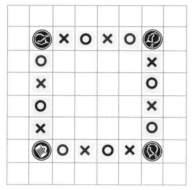

Player 1 begins by sliding any one piece one space horizontally or vertically; diagonal moves are not allowed.

Three Possible First Moves

→

Two Illegal First Moves (Pieces Slide Diagonally)

Player 2 then moves in a similar fashion. After the first two moves, a fascinating pair of complications come into play:

String Theory

All playing pieces—including the four anchors—must be considered beads along a string. After each move, the string can form a loop or a single strand, but any move that "snips" the string into *two* strands is illegal.

A Single Strand

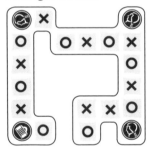

A Single Loop

Illegal Formations: 2 Strands

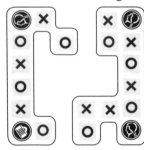

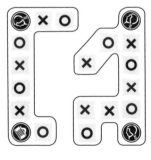

Jumping

Instead of sliding a piece on his turn, a player may opt to jump one of his pieces over a neighboring piece. Only a single piece may be jumped, and the space beyond the jumped piece must be empty in order to accept a jumper. Only horizontal and vertical jumps are allowed, not diagonals. Players can jump opponent pieces, anchor pieces, or their own pieces.

→ If a player jumps an opponent's piece, he must either flip the jumped piece or flip the piece that made the jump.

→ If a player jumps one of his own pieces or an anchor piece, nothing is flipped.

HOW TO WIN

A player wins when any move—his own or an erroneous move by his opponent—results in any three of his markers being simultaneously same-side-up and consecutively aligned (horizontally, vertically, or diagonally).

Three Winning Positions

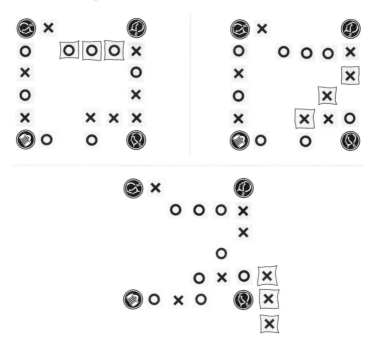

→

Remember: Three in a row diagonally is a winning position, but you may never move pieces diagonally.

NOTE

Stalemates are possible in Moka. If you get into a situation where both players are repetitively looping through a sequence of moves, you may decide to call a tie and start a new game.

METAXO

It sounds like a brand of tequila and is arguably more fun when played while imbibing, but Metaxo actually stands for "Meta Tic-Tac-Toe": It's a way to combine Tic-Tac-Toe with any other competitive two-player game. In fact, you can combine it with up to nine different games, turning Tic-Tac-Toe into a ten-in-one tournament. It's a great game for team play as well. Depending on your preferences, a single round of Metaxo can be played over an hour, a day, a week, or a year!

SETUP

Draw a traditional Tic-Tac-Toe grid. Choose nine other games from this book. Write the names of the nine games on individual scraps of paper and put them in a bag, hat, cup, or other container.

HOW TO PLAY

Player 1 points to a square on the Tic-Tac-Toe grid and pulls a scrap from the bag. The players must now compete at whatever game is drawn. The winner of that game makes her mark on the chosen Tic-Tac-Toe square.

Next, Player 2 selects another square and pulls another scrap. The game ends when one player captures three squares in a row on the Tic-Tac-Toe grid.

Gourmet Grandma	Battleship	Cryptar
Bongo	Wordcore	Gravilex
Ghost	Meta-Boxes	Sliders

NIM

In 1961, director Alan Resnais released the surreal romance *Last Year at Marienbad,* in which two lovers repeatedly play a simple game involving rows of matchsticks. As it turns out, the name of the Marienbad game—which can easily be played with only pen and paper—is Nim. Versions of Nim have been played for thousands of years across several continents. Play the game a few dozen times, and you'll begin feel like you're on the surreal verge of understanding some profound system of logic. In fact, you are! (See box, opposite page.)

SETUP

Draw a series of rows of vertical lines. You can draw any number of rows, each of which can contain as many lines as you wish.

```
/ / / / / / / / /
/ / / / / / / / / / / / /
/ / / / /
/ / / / / / / / / /
/ / / / /
/ / / / / / / / / / /
```

OBJECT OF THE GAME

To cross out the final mark in an ever-dwindling array.

HOW TO PLAY

Player 1 crosses out any number of lines within a single row. At least one line must be crossed out. For example, the following are all legitimate moves:

```
/ / / / / / / / /
/++/ / / / / / / / / / /
/ / / / /
/ / / / / / / / / /
/ / / / /
/ / / / / / / / / / / /
```

```
/ / / / / / / / /
/ / / / / / / / / / / / /
/ / / / /
/ / /++/ / / / /
/ / / / /
/ / / / / / / / / / /
```

```
/ / / / / / / / /
/ / / / / / / / / / / / /
/++/
/ / / / / / / / / /
/ / / / /
/ / / / / / / / / / / /
```

```
/ / / / / / / / /
/ / / / / / / / / / /++/ /
/ / / / /
/ / / / / / / / / /
/ / / / /
/ / / / / / / / / / /
```

Player 2 does the same, and play alternates until the final mark is crossed out. The player who crosses out the final mark wins.

VARIATION

Simply play with the reverse goal: The player who crosses out the final mark loses.

IS THERE REALLY A WINNING SYSTEM?

Well, yes. But, as in Tic-Tac-Toe, you've got to be the first player to make a move to guarantee a win. More important, you've got to be a math whiz to put the system into practice. The winning Nim strategy involves a complex series of speedy mental calculations, including the conversion of the number of marks in each row of the initial setup into binary numbers. It's said that there are Nim hustlers in India who can effortlessly perform these sophisticated operations in their heads; they work the streets like Three-Card Monte dealers.

→

An excellent article by Alexander Bogomolny containing a round-up of academic Nim system analyses can be found on the Mathematical Association of America's website (www.maa.org). If you have a truly nim-ble mind, getting a grip on Nim may help you understand the underpinnings of several other games in this book. Of course, if you'd rather play games than ponder complex theories for the next few hours, just turn the page and carry on!

If you're a math maniac, try figuring out the relationship between winning strategies for Nim and for:

DOTS AND DOODLES
SPROUTS

Invented in 1967 by mathematicians John Conway and Michael Paterson at Cambridge University, Sprouts has been puzzled over and theorized about for nearly four decades. It's been written about in *Scientific American* and studied by a think tank at Bell Labs. Yet despite the fact that it's both incredibly easy to play and endlessly fascinating, Sprouts has never really made the leap from the academic community to the general public. This may change, of course, once you begin to challenge your friends . . .

SETUP
Mark a piece of paper with three or more randomly placed dots.

OBJECT OF THE GAME
To be the last player able to grow a sprout in an increasingly tangled thicket.

HOW TO PLAY
Player 1 draws a "sprout": a line connecting any dot to any other dot. It can be long and winding or very short. At a place of her choosing along this line, Player 1 draws a new dot.

There are four rules governing the drawing of sprouts:

→ Each sprout must connect two dots.

→ A sprout may not cross any existing sprouts.

→ Every time a sprout is drawn, a new dot must be placed somewhere along its length.

→ A dot may be contacted by a maximum of three sprouts. (When a new dot is placed along a new sprout, it instantly has two of its three contacts used up.)

→

Player 2 now draws a sprout. Players alternate turns until one player cannot draw a viable sprout.

SAMPLE GAME

Beginning with three dots, here's each step of a sample game.

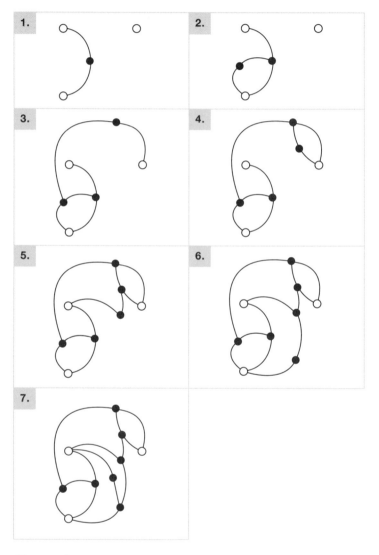

Player 1 wins!

> "Sprouts is an intellectual game that has had an underground popularity with scientists for a number of years. The rules are simple. All you do is connect the dots."
>
> —Science fiction author Piers Anthony
>
> from the novel *Macroscope* (1969)

VARIATION

Sprouts Plus!

The rules are the same as in the basic game, but instead of starting with dots, start with + signs. On each turn, a player draws a sprout that connects an arm of one + to an arm of a different +, drawing a single + at any point along the sprout, effectively creating two new arms. The winner is the last player able to draw a viable sprout.

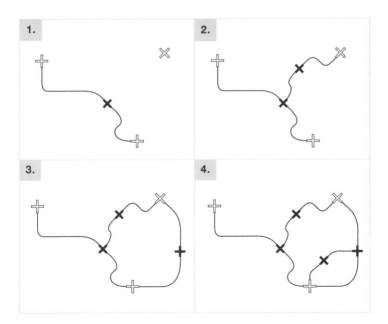

→

5.

6.

7.

8.

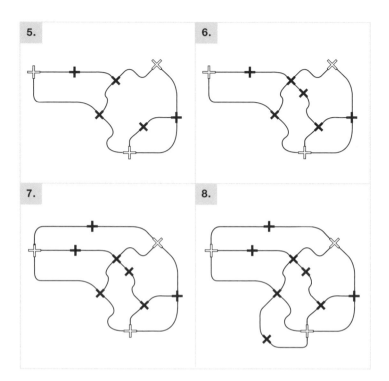

Final Move

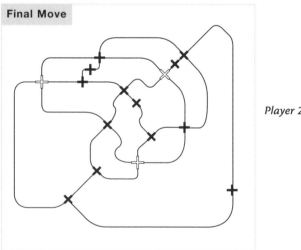

Player 2 wins!

LOOPERMAN

The bigger the paper you use and the more dots you start with, the loopier this cousin of Sprouts (see page 65) becomes. When playing a giant game, you may want to give each player a different colored pen to make it easier to look back and do a strategy analysis after the game.

SETUP

Draw any number of dots on a piece of paper.

OBJECT OF THE GAME

To draw the last possible loop.

HOW TO PLAY

Players alternate turns. On each turn, a player must draw a loop that passes through one or two dots. No loops may touch or cross.

HOW TO WIN

The last player who can make a legitimate loop wins.

SAMPLE MOVES

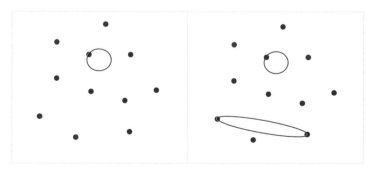

Loop passes through one dot.   *Loop passes through two dots.*

→

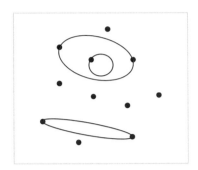

Loop surrounds another loop (often a good strategy!)

ILLEGAL MOVES

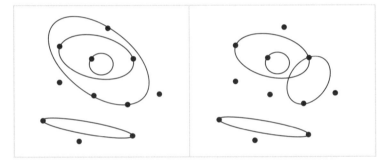

Loop passes through three dots.   *Loop touches another loop.*

VARIATIONS

Last Loop Loses

The player who makes the final possible loop loses.

Looperman at Large

When playing with a large number of dots, increase the maximum number of dots a loop is allowed to pass through.

DOTS AND BOXES

Don't avoid this one because you remember how easy it was to play when you were a little kid. By applying some strategic thinking and adding some new twists to the rules, you can turn Dots and Boxes into a serious brainteasing challenge. One mathematics professor, Elwyn Berlekamp of the University of California at Berkeley, has actually published a book-length scholarly study of the game. Think of the basic rules and variations below as a starter kit; once you learn them, you can mix and match the rules to generate even more complex versions.

SETUP

Draw a rectangular grid of dots. Rows and columns can be of any length, but dots must be clearly aligned and should be spaced approximately 1/4 inch or 1 cm apart. Graph paper is extremely useful for this!

OBJECT OF THE GAME

To complete the drawing of more square boxes than your opponent.

HOW TO PLAY

Player 1 draws a short line segment connecting any one dot to its closest neighbor horizontally or vertically.

Player 2 does the same. Player 2's segment does not have to touch Player 1's segment, though it can. Play rotates through all players, with each drawing a single segment on her turn. Whenever a player draws a segment that completes the fourth side of a square box, she marks the box with her initial.

→

For example, on Player 2's fifth move, she completed a square and marked it.

HOW TO WIN

When the grid is completely connected by line segments, play stops and players add up the number of boxes they have initialed. The player with the most initialed boxes wins.

VARIATIONS

Each of these superficially simple additions to the rules has major strategic implications for thoughtful players. The first or second variation can be combined with the third to complicate things further!

Non-Stop Dots

Whenever a player completes and initials a square, she takes another turn and draws another line segment immediately. This sometimes allows a player to form several boxes before the next player gets her turn.

Option Dots

When a player completes and initials a square, she can choose to take another turn and draw another line segment immediately or to pass the turn to the next player.

Locked Boxes

If a player has the opportunity to complete a box on her turn, she *must* do so. If there are several three-sided boxes ready for completion, the player has her choice of any one.

TRI-DOTS

Double the fun of Dots and Boxes by allowing diagonal lines to be drawn as well. See Dots and Boxes (page 71) for a refresher on how to play the basic game. Instead of scoring for completed boxes, however, the goal is to complete 1 x 1 x 1 right triangles. Players should each use a different colored pen, because triangles will overlap. There are four possible right triangles in each box (only two can be used). When played on a 10 x 10 grid, there are a total of 200 points to be won in a game of Tri-Dots.

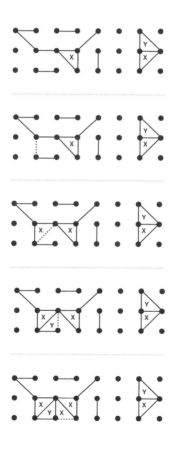

META-BOXES

Here's a way to complicate basic Dots and Boxes considerably, adding many new scoring opportunities. See Dots and Boxes (page 71) for the basic instructions. Points are scored not only for the completion of the smallest boxes within the grid, but all for *all* square units within the grid.

When Player Y draws the line to complete the small square below, he is simultaneously completing a larger 2 x 2 square. Player Y scores 2 points for this move, one for each completed square.

Rather than counting up initials at the end of the round, an ongoing point tally should be kept throughout the game. Players can claim any of the 1 x 1 boxes, 2 x 2 boxes, 3 x 3 boxes, and so on.

In a game of basic Dots and Boxes on a 10 x 10 grid, a total of 81 points will be distributed among the players. In a game of Meta-Boxes on a 10 x 10 grid, there are 285 points up for grabs!

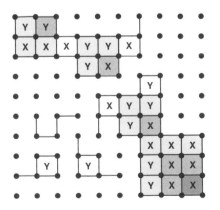

TRAILBLAZER

In this quick and easy game, opponents are, quite literally, at cross purposes. One player tries to move across a vertical grid while the other tries to traverse a horizontal grid. The two grids, however, are interlocked and the two paths are forbidden to intersect. It's important to think defensively as well as offensively.

SETUP

Draw a grid of dots with one more column than rows. For example: 8 columns by 7 rows. Draw an intersecting grid with the inverse measurements: 7 columns by 8 rows. Avoid confusion by using a different color of ink to draw each grid. Graph paper makes this much easier!

OBJECT OF THE GAME

To create a trail that crosses your grid without being blocked by your opponent.

→

HOW TO PLAY

Player 1 chooses a grid and draws a line segment connecting any two neighboring dots on that grid. Segments may only be horizontal or vertical, not diagonal.

Player 2 draws a line segment connecting any two neighboring dots on the other grid.

Play alternates in this fashion. Players may not draw across segments drawn by the other player.

HOW TO WIN

The first player to complete a trail of line segments that extends from one short side to the other on his grid is the winner.

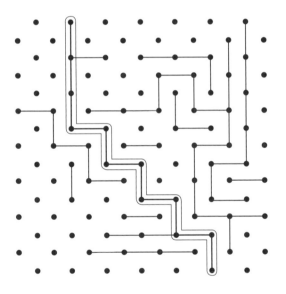

Player in red wins!

GRIDLOCK

Until now, you've never seen a bumper sticker exhorting you to "Honk If You Love Gridlock!" but after playing this game a bit, you may want to create one. However, this game should probably be avoided on car trips—it could be a bad omen. The goal of the game is to create an impossible-to-navigate traffic jam, forcing your opponent to stall out and not be able to make any more moves. It uses the same layout as Dots and Boxes (see page 71), but demands an entirely different strategic approach.

SETUP

Draw a rectangular grid of dots. Rows and columns can be of any length, but dots must be clearly aligned and should be spaced approximately ¼ inch or 1 cm apart. Graph paper is extremely useful for this!

OBJECT OF THE GAME

To lock up the playing grid so your opponent cannot make a move.

HOW TO PLAY

Player 1 begins by drawing either a horizontal or a vertical line segment that connects any two neighboring dots. If she draws a horizontal segment, she must continue to make horizontal segments on each subsequent turn, and Player 2 can draw only vertical segments on her turns.

Player 2 draws a line segment (vertically or horizontally, depending on which Player 1 has chosen) that connects any two dots *but does not touch another line segment*. Play alternates back and forth.

Legal Moves

→

Illegal Moves

HOW TO WIN

When a player cannot draw an acceptable line segment, the other player wins the game.

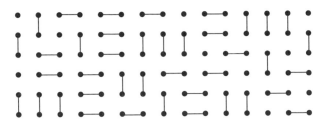

Player in red wins!

BATTLESHIP

"You sunk my battleship!"

For Americans who grew up in the 1970s, the shouted advertising slogan for Milton Bradley's game of naval maneuvers is as nostalgic as a *Brady Bunch* re-run . . . and just as plastic, too. Battleship is a classic example of a pen-and-paper game being transformed into molded polymers and sold to a public that had previously played for free.

Now, in the grand tradition of *Raise the Titanic* and the salvage of the Bismarck, its time to pull pen-and-paper Battleship back to the surface of cultural consciousness. It's fun, it's free, and it's the end of losing pesky little pegs between the sofa cushions. Early pen-and-paper Battleship was actually more challenging than the 1970s toy version, which was simplified so it could be marketed to children. Here are rules for both the familiar game and the intriguing original.

SETUP

Each player marks off two 17 x 17 grids on a sheet of paper. (Graph paper is extremely useful!) The upper left corner of each grid is left blank. The remaining squares of the upper row are labeled A through P, and the remaining squares of the leftmost column are labeled 1 through 16.

Each player then positions a fleet of ships on one of his grids by outlining the appropriate number of squares.

The fleet consists of:

1 AIRCRAFT CARRIER: 5 squares long, ⬚⬚⬚⬚⬚

1 BATTLESHIP: 4 squares, ⬚⬚⬚⬚

1 DESTROYER: 3 squares, ⬚⬚⬚

2 CRUISERS: 2 squares each, ⬚⬚ and ⬚⬚

1 SUBMARINE: 1 square, ⬚

As long as both players agree, any number of additional ships may be added to each fleet.

→

Ships are placed anywhere on the grid horizontally or vertically, but not diagonally.

	A	B	C	D	E	F	G	H	I	J	K	L	M	N	O	P
1																
2																
3																
4																
5																
6																
7																
8																
9																
10																
11																
12																
13																
14																
15																
16																

OBJECT OF THE GAME

To locate and sink your opponent's fleet of ships.

HOW TO PLAY: 1970S STYLE GAME

Player 1 "takes a shot" by calling out the alpha-numeric coordinates of one square on Player 2's Fleet Grid (e.g., B-4 or G-12).

Player 2 responds by revealing whether that coordinate represents a **HIT** (a portion of a ship occupies that square) or a **MISS** (the square is unoccupied).

Now Player 2 calls a shot and Player 1 responds. The shots continue to alternate in this fashion.

Players keep track of their own **HITS** and **MISSES** on their second, shipless Strike Grids, effectively building a map of the opponent's Fleet Grid and trying to deduce ship locations. Mark **HITS** with **X**s and **MISSES** with **O**s.

When a player scores a HIT, the opponent **X**s out that square of his Fleet Grid. When the last remaining square of a ship is **HIT,** the opponent must announce the sinking of that particular ship (e.g., "You sunk my battleship!").

HOW TO WIN

A player wins by sinking his opponent's entire fleet.

NOTE

For faster play, whenever a player scores a **HIT,** he gets to take another shot immediately. Only when a player misses does the other player begin to shoot.

TIP

Until you've got some **HIT**s and have begun to hone in on ship locations, don't waste shots by calling two adjacent coordinates (A-1 and A-2, or A-1 and B-1). Since all ships except the submarine are at least two squares long, your early shots are more deductively effective if you space them apart by at least one coordinate.

HOW TO PLAY: OLD ORIGINAL GAME

On each turn, a player gets to take one shot for each unsunk ship in his fleet. So, in the first turn, Player 1 announces six shots. For example:

A-1, A-3, A-5, B-2, B-4, B-6

Player 2 responds by telling Player 1 if any hits were scored but doesn't reveal *which* shots yielded the hits. If there were any hits, Player 1 marks all six coordinates as a **HIT ZONE.**

As play alternates, players keeps a record of **MISS ZONES** and **HIT ZONES** on their Strike Grids, building a "sonar map" of likely enemy positions. Mark **HIT ZONES** with **X**s and **MISS ZONES** with **O**s.

As in the 1970s-style game, each player **X**s out squares in the ships

→

when their coordinates are hit. But when a ship is finally announced as sunk—"You sunk my cruiser!"—its exact position remains unrevealed to the opponent.

Each time a player loses a ship, her number of shots per turn is reduced by one. So, with two ships sunk, a player gets only four shots per turn instead of six.

Here's a snapshot of a sample game.

Player 1's Fleet Grid

	A	B	C	D	E	F	G	H	I	J	K	L	M	N	O	P
1																
2															O	
3					O											
4				O	X	O		O		O						
5			O		O	X	X	X	O	X	O					
6					X	X	X	O	X	O	X					
7					X	X	X	X	X	X	X	X				
8								O		O						
9									O		O					
10									O		O					
11																
12			O				O									
13																
14																
15																
16																

ROUND	PLAYER 2'S CALLS	PLAYER 1'S RESPONSES
1	E-4, E-6, F-5, F-7, H-6, I-7	HIT
2	H-5, I-6, J-5, J-7, K-6, L-7	HIT
3	I-8, I-10, J-9, K-8, K-10, L-9	MISS
4	H-4, H-6, I-5, J-4, J-6, K-5	MISS
5	E-7, F-6, G-5, G-7, H-7, K-7	You SUNK my aircraft carrier!
6	C-5, D-4, E-3, E-5, F-4	MISS

Player 1's Strike Grid

	A	B	C	D	E	F	G	H	I	J	K	L	M	N	O	P
1										X						
2										X	X	X	X			
3										X	X	X	X			
4		O						O		X						
5										X						
6										X		O				
7				O											X	
8											O		O	X	O	
9												X				
10				O							O	X			O	
11					O					X				O		
12				O												
13			O													
14		O														
15	O															
16																

ROUND	PLAYER 1'S CALLS	PLAYER 2'S RESPONSES
1	D-7, F-10, H-4, L-6, N-11, B-4	MISS
2	K-2, K-3, L-2, L-3, M-2, M-3	HIT
3	J-1, J-2, J-3, J-4, J-5, J-6	You SUNK my cruiser!
4	A-15, B-14, C-13, D-12, E-11	MISS
5	K-11, L-10, M-9, N-8, O-7	HIT
6	K-8, K-10, L-8, O-8, O-10	MISS

Player 1 started out with a random hit zone, then started working in more consistent shapes. Turn the page to get a look at Player 2's Fleet Grid, to see how close Player 1 was getting!

→

Player 2's Fleet Grid

HOW TO WIN

A player wins when his opponent's entire fleet has been sunk. At this point, the locations of the sunken ships is revealed.

NOTE

For faster play, rather than getting one shot per turn for each unsunk boat in their fleets, players get one shot for each unhit square in their fleets (see boat lengths, above). So, on Player 1's first turn, he would get 16 shots. If Player 2 took two **HITS** from Player 1's first fusillade, he would only have 14 shots on his first turn.

TIPS

→ Because the exact coordinates of **HIT**s are never revealed, you can potentially confuse your opponent by placing pairs of ships close to each other.

→ Early fusillades of shots are most effective if used to help start carving the grid into densely packed **HIT ZONES** and **DEAD ZONES:** Consider firing in checkerboard style patches (A-1, B-2, A-3, C-1, C-3) or in diagonal lines (A-1, B-2, C-3, D-4, E-5).

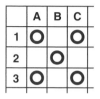

	A	B	C
1	O		O
2		O	
3	O		O

	A	B	C	D	E
1	O				
2		O			
3			O		
4				O	
5					O

BATTLESHIP AND THE TIDE OF TECHNOLOGY	
WORLD WAR I	Russian soldiers develop early Battleship-style games to pass time in the field. They use whatever writing implements and paper are handy.
1930s	Boardless Battleship-style games called Broadsides, Combat, and Salvo are published in pen and pencil versions. The grids are pre-printed and sold as pads.
1967	Milton Bradley introduces the famous plastic incarnation of Battleship, with hundreds of tiny, easy-to-lose pieces.
1983	Electronic Battleship brings blinking lights and sound effects to the original Milton Bradley version.
1990s	Minesweeper, a human vs. computer variation of Battleship, is included with Microsoft Windows software.
1998	The CD-ROM game Battling Ships is released by Sierra On-Line, Inc. (Many free Battleship games can be found on the Internet.)
2004	*Gladstone's Games to Go* brings back the good old days!

CODEWORD

Also known as Jotto™, this is a classic reasoning game that takes serious focus. It's no mere time-killer; close attention is a must. Endlessly diverting for adult players, CodeWord is also a great way to teach kids how to think deductively—just make sure to choose secret words that are at an appropriate vocabulary level!

OBJECT OF THE GAME

To guess your opponent's secret word.

HOW TO PLAY

Player 1 secretly chooses a four-letter CodeWord according to the following criteria and writes it down on a piece of paper.

→ Proper nouns are not allowed. Pick **ROME** and you'll be sent wandering in search of another choice. Pick **ROAM** and you're magnifico!

→ The CodeWord must have four distinct letters, no repeats. Pick **BALE** and you're ready to play. Pick **BALL** and reveal yourself to be a hayseed.

→ Contractions are forbidden. Don't choose **DON'T.**

Player 2 makes a guess at the CodeWord, according to the following criteria.

→ Guesses, unlike CodeWords, are allowed to include repeated letters. **KOOK** is OK!

→ Guesses must be real words, not random letter sequences. **DODO** is fine, but **LOLO** is a no-no.

After Player 2 writes down her guess, Player 1 gives the guess a mark between 0 and 4, corresponding to the number of letters shared by the guess word and the CodeWord. The position of the letters is not a factor. For example:

CODEWORD	GUESS	MARK
GIRL	TWIG	2
GIRL	GIST	2
KNOT	SINK	2
ROTS	HOOD	1
TARP	PANT	3

In the fourth example, note that ROTS and HOOD only share one letter in common, a single O. The additional O in the guess word is simply ignored.

Player 2 continues to guess and be marked by Player 1 until the CodeWord is correctly guessed. For example, if the CodeWord were DARK, here's how the game could progress:

GUESS	MARK
DOGS	1
BOOK	1
DADS	2
BAGS	1
SAGS	1
GAGS	1
DODO	1
PARK	3
PORK	2
DARK	Correct!

Player 2's score for the round is the number of guesses it took to arrive at the CodeWord. In this case, the score is 10.

Next, Player 2 picks a CodeWord and Player 1 attempts to figure out what it is.

HOW TO WIN

The player who uses the least number of total guesses to crack four CodeWords is the winner.

→

VARIATIONS

→ Change the marking system—and speed up the game—by giving more detailed feedback, including information on the *positions* of common letters. For example, for a CodeWord of **GIRL:**

GUESS	MARK USING BASIC RULES	MARK USING VARIATION RULES
TWIG	2	0, 2 (no common letters in common positions, 2 common letters)
GIST	2	2, 0 (two common letters in common positions, no additional common letters)
WIGS	2	1, 1 (one common letter in a common position, one additional common letter)

→ Use five-letter CodeWords and guesses.

→ Disallow the use of pen and paper by the code-breaking player, forcing her to keep track of guesses in her head. (The code-making player should maintain a written record of the guesses in case there are scoring disputes.)

PRACTICE PUZZLERS

Can you crack the CodeWord on the next guess in each of these sample rounds? Answers are on page 144.

1.

GUESS	MARK
CRAB	0
CODE	2
HEED	2
DEED	1
HERO	3
HOME	3
POEM	3

2.

GUESS	MARK
CALM	1
CACA	0
LOOM	1
PEEL	2
KEEL	2
BILE	2
YULE	3
MULE	3
FUEL	3
RULE	3
DUEL	3
GLUE	3
AXLE	2

3.

GUESS	MARK
BANK	0
COME	1
CURD	0
GOLD	2
GOBS	3
LOG	3

CRYPTAR

Cryptar is quite similar to CodeWord (page 86), with one critical, cryptic twist: A familiarity with the English language won't help you! A plastic version of this game, played with colored pegs and a board, sold like hotcakes in the mid-1970s. It generated untold riches for Israeli postmaster Mordecai Meirowitz, who pitched the idea to more than a dozen toy companies before selling it to the British firm that ultimately marketed it as Mastermind® and sold over 55 million sets in more than 80 countries. The game's James Bond-style box-top, featuring a sultry model hovering over the shoulder of a dashing bearded supervillain, could be spotted in suburban homes everywhere. For a brief shining moment, nerdy braniac kids felt suave.

OBJECT OF THE GAME

To guess your opponent's secret code.

HOW TO PLAY

Player 1 secretly chooses and writes down a five-element code, consisting of any combination of the following six symbols:

> O ! ? X <

Repetition of symbols is allowed. A secret code could be **X X X X X**, or **>!>>!**

On a blank sheet of paper, Player 2 writes down a guess at the code:

X O X ? !

Player 1 marks the guess, using the detailed feedback system explained in the variation of CodeWord on page 88.

The round continues until Player 2 deduces the code. The game resumes with Player 2 generating a code and Player 1 guessing at it.

HOW TO WIN

The player who uses the least number of total guesses to crack four codes is the winner.

VARIATIONS

→ Increase the length the codes beyond five symbols.

→ Expand the pool of symbols from which codes are constructed. Add **/**, **=**, or **∧**, for instance.

GOLDEN RULE

Where Cryptar (see page 90) and CodeWord (see page 86) require deductive reasoning to crack specific codes, Golden Rule challenges players to use inductive reasoning to determine a governing principle that can generate numerous codes. In mystery lovers' terms, it's not about nailing a suspect, it's about figuring out a motive.

OBJECT OF THE GAME

To figure out the common element—the Golden Rule—that connects a group of words of three or more letters.

HOW TO PLAY

One player is selected as the Ruler for the round. She writes down a single rule that will be used to distinguish "good" words from "bad" words. The other players should each divide a blank piece of paper into two columns, labeled "good" and "bad."

Rules can relate to spelling, meaning, or sound. The more complicated the rules, the more challenging the game. Players should make an effort to invent rules that are challenging and creative as well as appropriate for the skill level of the group.

Examples of simple rules:

→ Words must begin with E (e.g., **ERA**, **EMERALD**, **ECTOPLASM**).

→ Words must be names of pro sports teams (e.g., **BEARS**, **CUBS**, **EAGLES**).

→ Words must include a hard K sound (e.g., **KILL**, **RICOCHET**, **LICK**).

Examples of more difficult rules:

→ Words must have an E within the first three letters (e.g., **ECTOPLASM**, **CREPT**, **BELFRY**, **ARE**).

→ Words must be associated with sports (e.g., **LOSE**, **BASKET**, **LEAGUE**, **CHEER**).

➜ Words must begin and end with the same sound (e.g., **MOM**, **CRANK**, **NOCTURNE**).

Examples of complex rules:

➜ Words must have E as their second letter and D as their last (e.g., **BED**, **TETHERED**, **WESTWARD**).

➜ Words must contain a pair of letters in the same order they appear in the alphabet (e.g., **ABSTRACT**, **BEARS**, **FRIGHTENING**, **CABIN**).

After the Golden Rule for the round has been recorded, the Ruler announces a pair of words, one good and one bad, to the other players. (The Ruler must work within her head after writing down the Rule, but the other players may take notes.)

Moving clockwise around the group, players propose words, which the Ruler deems good or bad. Each time a player's word is deemed good, the player has the option of taking a guess at the Rule. Because wrong guesses are penalized, players may sometimes choose not to exercise this option.

When there is an incorrect guess at the Rule, the Ruler must announce a word that is good under her Rule but bad under the rule proposed by the player in order to exemplify why the proposed rule is incorrect.

The round is over when the Rule is guessed correctly.

Here's a short sample game:

RULER	GREEN is good. DIRT is bad.
PLAYER 1	YELLOW
RULER	Bad
PLAYER 2	BLUE
RULER	Bad
PLAYER 3	RED
RULER	Bad
PLAYER 1	PURPLE
RULER	Bad
PLAYER 2	SPLEEN

→

RULER	Good.
PLAYER 2	I want to guess. The Rule is "Words must include two Es in a row."
RULER	You are incorrect. ENGINE is good.
PLAYER 3	GRAY
RULER	Bad
PLAYER 1	EVEN
RULER	Good
PLAYER 1	I want to guess. The Rule is, "Words must contain at least two Es."
RULER	That is incorrect. IMAGINE is good.
PLAYER 2	OVER
RULER	Bad
PLAYER 3	NEVER
RULER	Good
PLAYER 3	I want to guess. The Rule is "Words must contain at least one N."
RULER	You are correct!

If playing for points (see below), each player must get to be Ruler in an equal number of rounds.

SCORING

The initial value of guessing the Golden Rule in any round is 1 point. Each time a player makes a wrong guess, the value of the Golden Rule goes up by a point. If there have been four wrong guesses and the next guess is correct, the player making that correct guess wins 5 points, ending the round.

The Ruler is awarded the same number of points as the correct guesser each round.

A wrong guess incurs a loss of 1 point.

The scoring for the sample round above would be:

PLAYER 1	–1 POINT
PLAYER 2	–1 POINT
PLAYER 3	3 POINTS
RULER	3 POINTS

If, after any guess, the Ruler cannot come up with a word that is good under her Golden Rule and bad under the guesser's proposed rule, the current value of a correct guess is deducted from the Ruler's score and the round is ended.

NOTES & NIT-PICKS

→ To encourage precision and avoid disagreements, Rules should include quantifying terms such as "at least" and "exactly" whenever appropriate. Under the Rule "Words must contain an O," it would be unclear whether NOODLE was good or bad. But there would be no confusion if the Rule was either "Words must contain exactly one O" (in which case NOODLE would be bad) or "Words must contain at least one O" (in which case NOODLE would be good).

→ In the case of disagreements, the broadest interpretation of the Rule prevails.

VARIATION

Experienced groups can try playing with sentences instead of words, allowing grammar and punctuation to be figured into the Rule. Games take more time and require more concentration.

Sample rules for play with sentences:

→ Sentences must contain exactly one past-tense verb.

→ Sentences must include at least one comma and one proper noun.

→ Sentences must contain exactly one word that begins with O and no four-letter words.

If you enjoy the sentence version of Golden Rule, try Ex Post Facto (see page 96).

EX POST FACTO

If you're the type who likes to make up the rules as you go along, here's your ideal game. After generating a hodgepodge of unrelated sentences, players impose their own sense of order to try and make sense of the mess. In Ex Post Facto, the end justifies the means!

Ex Post Facto is a sort of evil twin to Golden Rule (see page 92). Playing each will improve your skill at the other.

OBJECT OF THE GAME

To generate as many laws as possible that apply to every example in a random group of sentences.

HOW TO PLAY

Each player writes a single sentence on a piece of paper. The players' sentences are passed around the group so that everyone can copy down each one.

Once everyone has written down all the sentences, a designated timekeeper calls "Start." Each player then has three minutes to come up with as many absolute laws as possible that apply to every sentence in the batch. Laws can apply to spelling, word order, grammar, punctuation, and any other patterns players might identify.

Here are three sentences, followed by some of the laws that could be made to describe them:

Sentences

The quick brown fox jumps over the lazy dog.

You are what you eat.

Hurry, before your time runs out!

Some Applicable Laws

→ Sentences must end with a consonant.

→ The last two letters of each sentence must be a vowel, then a consonant.

→ Sentences must include at least one Y.

➔ Sentences must include at least one word that ends in a consonant and is followed by a word that begins with a consonant (brown fox; what you; hurry before).

Restrictions on Laws

Laws must address common attributes, not deficits. The following would be unacceptable as laws to describe the sentences in the sample group above:

➔ Sentences must not include the word "zebra."

➔ Sentences must not include more than one comma.

Laws that include different phrases but mean the same thing are not different laws. The following two laws are equivalent:

➔ Sentences must include at least one Y.

➔ Sentences must include one or more Ys.

Laws may not include "or" conditions. The following law would not be acceptable:

➔ Sentences must end with a B or a D.

Laws referring to quantities must be as precise as possible. Given the sentences in the above example, this would be an acceptable law:

➔ Sentences must contain two or more Es.

But these laws would not be acceptable:

➔ Sentences must contain an E.

➔ Sentences must contain one or more Es.

SCORING

At the end of the allotted three minutes, players read their laws to the group. The group may discuss the validity of any questionable law. Disputes are settled by majority rule. Ties are broken by the lawmaker.

Valid laws that appear on only one player's list score 2 points. Identical and equivalent laws shared by more than one player score 1 point. The player with the most points wins.

Despite a morbid metaphor at its core, this classic pen-and-pencil game has had an incredibly vital recent history. In 1975, it was transformed into the TV show *Wheel of Fortune*, originally hosted by Chuck Woolery, with letters turned by hostess Susan Stafford. Still going strong as one of the most successful syndicated television shows of all time, *Wheel of Fortune* has spun-off board games, battery-powered games, and computer games. But despite the dazzling entertainment value of current hosts Pat Sajak and Vanna White, *Wheel* truly owes its appeal to the little dead stickman of yore.

SETUP

Designate one person as the hangman. She draws an adorable little gallows and a series of blanks corresponding to a secret word she has chosen.

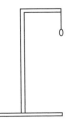

OBJECT OF THE GAME

To guess the hangman's secret word before you are figuratively asphyxiated.

HOW TO PLAY

Player 1, the hangman, thinks of a secret word, phrase, or short quotation and jots an arrangement of corresponding blanks beside the gallows. For example:

ARCHIPELAGO would be jotted as _ _ _ _ _ _ _ _ _ _ _

PIE IN THE SKY would be jotted as _ _ _   _ _   _ _ _   _ _ _

As in all word games, it's appropriate to use secret words that will be familiar to your opponents. Showing respect for others' vocabulary levels is a basic element of fair play.

Player 2 guesses a letter she thinks might be in the word. If the guessed letter is part of the secret word, Player 1 fills in each instance of that letter in the appropriate blank. For example, if Player 2 guesses "**A**" and the word is **ARCHIPELAGO**, Player 1 would fill in *both* **A**s:

A _ _ _ _ _ _ _ **A** _ _

If the guessed letter is *not* part of the word, Player 1 draws the head of a hanging victim on the gallows and writes the letter down in a discard pool.

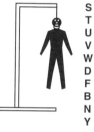

Play continues to one of three possible end points:

→ Player 2 successfully guesses all of the letters; the blanks of the secret word are completely filled in.

→ Player 2 correctly guesses the secret word before all of the letters are filled in.

→ Player 2 makes ten wrong guesses and the hanging body is completed. The 10 body parts are 1 head, 1 trunk, 2 arms, 2 legs, 2 eyes, 1 nose, 1 mouth.

Next, players switch roles and play another round. A game must include an even number of rounds.

SCORING

You can simply award one point to a guessing player whenever she solves the secret word and one point to an opposing player whenever a hanging body is completed.

A more complex scoring system follows:

Successfully filling in all the blanks	+1 POINT
Successfully guessing the secret word with less than half of the blanks filled in	+4 POINTS
Successfully guessing the secret word with half or more of the blanks filled in	+2 POINTS

Making a wrong guess at the secret word (a round is not ended by a wrong guess)	–2 POINTS
Making 10 wrong letter guesses and hanging	–4 POINTS

VARIATIONS

Well-Hung Man

Add one more choice body part and allow up to 11 wrong letter guesses.

Dueling Danglers

Instead of one guesser and one executioner in each round, each player assumes both roles simultaneously. Two gallows are drawn. Each player thinks of a secret word and they alternate letter guesses. When a player makes a guess at a letter in the other player's word, she must fill in all instances of that letter in her own word as well. A player can only opt to guess her opponent's secret word immediately after making a successful letter guess.

BALANCE YOUR BRAIN POWER

Hangman tends to favor the left-brained, but it can be played in tandem with Tic-Tac-Toe games (see pages 48 to 53) or Dots and Boxes (see page 71), which tend to favor right-brainers. In addition to the appropriate Tic-Tac-Toe or Dots grid, each player draws a gallows and the blanks for a secret word.

The game starts with Player 1 guessing a letter in Player 2's word. If the letter is in the word, Player 1 gets to make a move in the Tic-Tac-Toe or Dots game. If the letter is not in the word, a body part is hung, and it's Player 2's turn.

Whenever a word is completely filled in or a hangman is completed, a new gallows and new secret word are created. There are no points scored in the hangman games, they simply serve as gatekeepers for making moves in the Dots and Tic-Tac-Toe games.

DOUBLET RACING

Doublet puzzles, also known as Word Ladders, were first popularized by Lewis Carroll, the author of *Alice in Wonderland*, *Jabberwocky*, and other literary works chock-full of wordplay. Carroll published a series of doublet puzzles in the original *Vanity Fair* magazine in 1872. Traditionally solved as a solitary pursuit, Doublets are at the heart of this multi-player game.

OBJECT OF THE GAME

To transform a Launch Word into a Target Word of the same length by changing a single letter at a time.

HOW TO PLAY

A round begins with one player designating a Launch Word. For instance, **BUSH.** A second player designates a Target Word of the same length: **GORE.**

Time is set at five minutes. All players now work on their own to transform the Launch Word to the Target Word in a series of steps.

At each step, any single letter of the preceding word may be changed to any other letter of the alphabet, but the result must be another legitimate word. (No proper nouns or contractions are allowed.)

BUSH	
BASH	Change U to A
BATH	Change S to T
BATE	Change H to E
BARE	Change T to R
BORE	Change A to O
GORE	Change B to G

A game can consist of a single round, an agreed upon number of rounds, or as many rounds as it takes to fill an allotted time.

→

SCORING

Doublet races are scored for players' overall efficiency, with points distributed for Solution, Speed, Conciseness, and Realism.

Solution

All players who reach the target by the end of the allotted five minutes score 1 point.

Speed

A player who reaches the target before the end of the allotted five minutes may call "Solved!" The other players continue to work toward a solution until the five minutes are up. If the early solver's solution path checks out when verified by the other players at the end of the round, he is awarded 1 speed bonus point.

Only one player may call an early solve in each round.

Conciseness

Any player who has reached the target in fewer steps than any other player is awarded bonus points equal to the difference in steps between his solution and the longest solution.

For example, Player 1 transforms **WARM** to **COLD** in one less step than Player 2. He earns 1 bonus point:

PLAYER 1	PLAYER 2
WARM	WARM
WARD	WORM
WORD	WORE
CORD	CORE
COLD	COLE
	COLD

In a game with more than two players, multiple players can score conciseness bonus points.

Realism

At any time during a round, a player who becomes convinced that there are zero transformation paths from the Launch Word to the Target Word may call out "Impossible!"

At this point, other players must announce agreement or disagreement. Agreeing players stop trying to reach a solution. Disagreeing players continue to work toward a solution.

If none of the disagreeing players have reached the target at the end of the five minute time period, the player who called "Impossible!" scores 2 points. Agreeing players each score 1 point.

If *any* of the disagreeing players have acceptably reached the target at the end of the five minutes, all disagreeing players score 1 point and those who have reached the target score 1 additional point on top of their standard solution point. The player who called "Impossible!" loses 3 points, and any agreeing players lose 2 points.

DOUBLET TROUBLESHOOTING

Of course, impossible rounds inevitably crop up now and then. These word choice tips will help you avoid untransformable pairs. Keep away from Launch Words and Target Words that:

➜ end in a consonant followed by a Y (FURRY, MANY)

➜ have Qs in them

➜ have more than two consonants in a row (LIGHT, TINGLE)

VARIATION

Scrambled Doublets

At each step of a word-pair transformation, this nifty twist gives players a choice: They can either change one letter or they can scramble the order of the letters in the existing word. For example, here are two ways a player could step forward from the same word:

CHANGE	SCRAMBLE
STALE	STALE
STOLE	LEAST

→

A change and a scramble cannot be made on the same turn.

Here's a path from **BUSH** to **GORE** that incorporates a scramble.

BUSH	
RUSH	Change
RUSE	Change
RUBE	Change
ROBE	Change
BORE	Scramble
GORE	Change

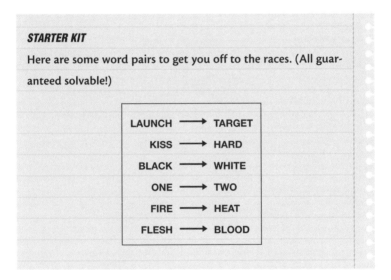

STARTER KIT

Here are some word pairs to get you off to the races. (All guaranteed solvable!)

LAUNCH ⟶ TARGET

KISS ⟶ HARD

BLACK ⟶ WHITE

ONE ⟶ TWO

FIRE ⟶ HEAT

FLESH ⟶ BLOOD

ATTACK OF THE CLONES

This is an extraordinarily challenging spin on Doublet Racing (see page 101). It should not be attempted by small children or the weak of brain. You'll want to be quite adept at both basic Doublet Racing and its scrambled variation before entering this mind-boggling linguistic battleground.

OBJECT OF THE GAME

To transform a Launch Word of three or more letters into a Target Word of three or more letters. The Launch Word and the Target Word do not have to have the same number of letters.

HOW TO PLAY

The rules and scoring are the same as in Doublet Racing, except that now there are four ways to make a step along the path from Launch to Target.

1 As in Doublet Racing, you can change a single letter.

   BARN

   BURN

2 As in Scrambled Doublets, you can rearrange the existing letters.

   SABER

   BEARS

3 You can clone one of the existing letters, which increases the length of the word.

   MOD

   MOOD

→

4 You are allowed to clone and scramble simultaneously in a single step.

MOD	RAGE
DOOM	EAGER

Zero path situations are much more common in this game than in standard Doublet Racing. It's advisable to have at least three players so that each round, one player can sit out and challenge the others with a word pair that he or she has already worked through. The player who presents the challenge is forbidden to offer a word pair for which a solution hasn't been found.

Here are two samples of cloning in action:

Launch Word: FEW

Target Word: MANY

Launch Word: BIG

Target Word: LOSER

FEW	
MEW	Change
MOW	Change
MOD	Change
MOOD	Clone
MOON	Change
MOAN	Change
MEAN	Change
MANE	Scramble
MANY	Change

BIG	
BOG	Change
NOG	Change
GOON	Clone and Scramble
GOOP	Change
GLOP	Change
SLOP	Change
POLLS	Clone and Scramble
POLES	Change
ROLES	Change
LOSER	Scramble

DOWNHILL RACER

The perfect portable game for après ski, Downhill Racer will keep your mind slaloming along as you give your body a break. It's the brainiac version of King of the Mountain!

SETUP

Players each write down an agreed upon summit of one vowel and one consonant.

OBJECT OF THE GAME

To make the most and steepest slopes of words, all descending from a fixed summit.

HOW TO PLAY

Each player has three minutes to create as many different slopes as he can, starting from the summit. Assign one player the role of timekeeper, and have him keep an eye on the clock.

Sample Slopes from a Summit of TI

SLOPE 1	SLOPE 2	SLOPE 3	SLOPE 4
TI	TI	TI	TI
TIE	TIN	TIP	TIE
TIME	TINS	TRIP	TILE
	TINTS	TRIPE	TILED
	TAINTS		

→

The rules for descending a slope are:

→ One letter must be added at each level.

→ With the exception of the summit, each level must consist of a real word.

→ The first letter in the summit must be the first letter of all words in the slope. Other letters need not remain consecutive, but they must remain in their initial order. In Slope 3 on the previous page, when **TIP** becomes **TRIP,** the order of the letters **T, I,** and **P** is preserved despite the insertion of the **R.** At the next level, an **A** could *not* be added to form **TAPIR,** because that would require re-ordering the letters.

→ Proper nouns are not permitted.

→ Pluralization is allowed in the midst of a slope, but the bottom-most word may not be the plural of the immediately preceding word. If Slope 2 above had ended at its third level, it would be disqualified, because **TINS** is the plural of the immediately preceding word, **TIN.** Likewise, if the fourth level were **TAINT,** the bottom level could not be **TAINTS,** as it is now.

SCORING

At the end of the allotted time, players compare their slopes and points are distributed. The steeper the slope, the more points:

2 LEVELS	1 POINT
3 LEVELS	2 POINTS
4 LEVELS	4 POINTS
5 LEVELS	8 POINTS
6+ LEVELS	16 POINTS

→ If two or more players have an identical slope (the same word at every level), the slopes cancel each other out.

→ If one player has a slope that is fully contained within another player's longer slope, the shorter slope is awarded no points. For example:

PLAYER 1	PLAYER 2
BA	**BA**
BAT	**BAT**
BATH	**BATH**
BATHS	
BATHES	
8 POINTS	**0 POINTS**

If Player 1 had both of the slopes above, the shorter slope would not count, as it is completely contained within another slope.

→ When two players have slopes of equal length that contain some identical levels, they are both awarded full points as long as at least one level does not match:

PLAYER 1	PLAYER 2
BA	**BA**
BAT	**BAT**
BATE	**BATH**
BATHE	**BATHE**
4 POINTS	**4 POINTS**

→ A player scores full points for each slope he created in which some, but not all, levels are identical.

PLAYER 1

BA	**BA**	**BA**	**BA**
BAT	**BAT**	**BAT**	**BAT**
BATE	**BAIT**	**BRAT**	**BEAT**

Player 1 would score a total of 8 points, 2 for each of these slopes.

→

SAMPLE GAME

Here's a scored sample round, starting from a summit of **TO**:

PLAYER 1

TO	TO	TO	TO	TO	TO
TOY	TOR	TOG	TOR	TOT	TOE
	TORT	TOGA	TOUR	TROT	TOED
	TORTE		TOURS	TROUT	TONED

1 + 4 + 2 + 0* + 4 + 4 = 15 points

PLAYER 2

TO	TO	TO	TO	TO	TO	TO
TON	TON	TOO	TOO	TOO	TOE	TON
TONS	TOWN	TOOT	TOOK	TOOL	TORE	TORN
TONES						THORN
						THORNY

4 + 2 + 2 + 2 + 2 + 2 + 8 = 22 points

VARIATION

To allow for steeper slopes, drop the rule requiring the first letter of the summit to be the first letter of all subsequent words.

TI	TI
TIP	TIN
TIPS	TINT
TRIPS	TINTS
STRIPS	STINTS
STRIPES	

If you enjoy Downhill Racer, check out Superghost (see page 21)!

* *Disqualified for plural last level.*

INITIALIST

In pursuit of a trivia game that doesn't favor particular players? Here's one in which every question can be tailored to showcase each competitor's personal expertise! The more eclectic your friends are, the more you'll learn every round. Literary snobs, movie buffs, science geeks, history mavens, and sports fans are always on equal footing. And, of course, there are no heavy boxes of cards to lug around.

SETUP

Choose two famous quotes, sentences from a handy book or magazine, or song lyrics:

> "Scaramouche, scaramouche, will you do the fandango?"
> > —Queen, "Bohemian Rhapsody"

> "Knights in white satin, never reaching the end . . ."
> > —The Moody Blues, "Knights in White Satin"

Each player writes the first ten letters of the two phrases in parallel columns, about an inch (3 cm) apart.

S	K
C	N
A	I
R	G
A	H
M	T
O	S
U	I
C	N
H	W

→

OBJECT OF THE GAME

To come up with the names of notable personalities whose names fit the given series of first and last initials.

HOW TO PLAY

When all players have finished setting up, the designated timer calls "Start." Players now have three minutes to match the columns' pairs of initials to notable people.

FIRST	LAST	WHO?
Sam	Kinison	Overwrought '80s comedian
Carrie	Nation	Nineteenth-century temperance crusader
Allen	Iverson	Basketball star
Robert	Guillaume	TV actor, *Benson*
Aldous	Huxley	Author, *Brave New World*
Mother	Theresa	Social worker in India
Oliver	Stone	Controversial film director
Ukelele	Ike	Folk singer (aka Cliff Edwards), voice of Jiminy Cricket in Walt Disney's *Pinnochio*
Chuck	Norris	Actor, *Walker, Texas Ranger*
Hank	Williams	Country music legend

"Notable people" is a debatable notion, and each group of players can decide whether any name is acceptable. Here are some general rules of thumb:

→ The player who names a person must be able to provide a brief description of the person.

→ Names must be sufficiently well-known that they could be found in a book or magazine on their field.

→ Fictional characters (**HOMER SIMPSON** for **H S, INDIANA JONES** for **I J**) are not acceptable unless ruled so by the group before the game begins.

→ Titles are allowed when they are part of the person's most commonly known identity. For example, **MISTER ROGERS** is an acceptable response to the initials **M R**, and the proper name **FRED ROGERS** would be an acceptable response to **F R**. Similarly acceptable: **COLONEL SANDERS** for **C S**, **HARLAN SANDERS** for **H S**; **DOCTOR RUTH** for **D R**, **RUTH WESTHEIMER** for **R W**. Unacceptable responses include **PRESIDENT BUSH** for **P B**, **SENATOR CLINTON** for **S C**.

HOW TO WIN

When time is up, players compare their lists and score them as follows:

→ Any player who has successfully filled in all of the initial pairs scores 2 points.

→ For each initial pair, each player who has come up with a unique name scores 1 point.

Highest score wins—or scores are carried over in a multiple round game.

VARIATIONS

Multiple Rounds

Play can be continued beyond a single round in one of several ways:

→ Choose two new phrases and generate new initial columns.

→ Invert the columns from the first round so that the first initials are now the last initials and vice versa.

→ Use the next ten letters from the two phrases that generated the first-round columns. (An epic game might work its way through the Gettysburg Address and the Declaration of Independence.)

The In Crowd

Extend the time limit from three to five minutes and try to find *as many famous names as possible* to match each set of initials. Scoring is the same as in the basic game, with the addition of the following bonus (to be tabulated prior to eliminating duplicate names):

→ 1 bonus point for the player with the highest number of acceptable names for an initial pair.

No bonus points are distributed for ties.

→

Catchphrases

Instead of famous names, use the initial columns to form compound words and common two-word phrases. For instance:

Duty	Calls
Over-	Achiever
Green	Thumb

If Catchphrases is your favorite version of Initialist, you'll also enjoy Chain Reaction (see page 23).

GLADSTONE GAMES!
GOODY GUMDROPS!
GIMME GIMME!
GIBLET GRAVY

PASSWORD

 One of the all-time greatest party games, Password requires an ingenious blend of logical thinking and creativity. Usually played in teams of two, it can also be played by a group of single competitors (details provided below). Password was adapted into an enormously successful TV game show hosted by Alan Ludden. Who was married to Betty White. Who was in *Golden Girls* with Bea Arthur. Who played Maude in a spin-off of *All in the Family*. Oops! Wrong game! (See Six Degrees, page 31.)

SETUP

Players get three scraps of paper apiece and write a password along with their initials on each scrap. The scraps are placed in a bag, hat, or cup.

OBJECT OF THE GAME

To guess a secret word—the password—based only on one-word clues provided by a teammate.

HOW TO PLAY

Player A from Team 1 selects one of the scraps. If the scrap is marked with his partner's initials, he returns it and selects another. He shows the word on the scrap to both members of Team 2, but not to his partner, Player B.

Player A now gives his partner a one-word clue to the password. For example, if the password were **SANDWICH**, the first clue might be **BREAD**.

Player B thinks of words related to the clue and tries to guess the secret word. He might guess **WHEAT**.

The exchange continues between Player A and Player B:

"The clue is BREAD."

    "Is the password WHEAT?"

"No. The clue is SUBMARINE."

    "Is the password ROLL?"

→

"No. The clue is HERO."

"Is the password SANDWICH?"

"Yes! You got it!"

All clues must meet the following criteria:

→ They must be only one word.

→ They cannot contain any part of the password. For example, **SCI-ENCE** cannot be used as a clue to **SCIENTIST,** and **HAM** cannot be used as a clue to **HAMMER.**

→ They cannot be accompanied by any sort of hand motion or pantomime.

→ They can be accompanied by informative facial expressions and verbal intonation. If **LEMON** was the password, the clue word **FRUIT** could be pronounced through tightly puckered lips.

→ They cannot rhyme with the password.

→ They can be presented only once.

A score is tallied after each round of clues and guesses.

SCORING

A team can score anywhere from 0 to 10 points for each password, depending on how many clues are required. The fewer the number of clues needed, the higher the score. The number of points and the number of clues are as follows:

CORRECT GUESS AFTER	POINTS
1 clue	10
2 clues	9
3 clues	8
4 clues	7
5 clues	6

CORRECT GUESS AFTER	POINTS
6 clues	5
7 clues	4
8 clues	3
9 clues	2
10 clues	1

If the password has not been guessed after 10 clues, the team scores zero, and the password is revealed.

HOW TO WIN

Play alternates between Team 1 and Team 2 and from player to player. Scores are totaled after 12 rounds to determine the winning team.

VARIATIONS

Censored Password

The rules are the same as the basic game, except that on the scraps of paper, players accompany each password with a list of three words that are forbidden as clues. For example, if the word were **HOSPITAL**, a player might list **DOCTOR, NURSE,** and **SURGERY** as off-limits clues.

Teamless Password (Four or More Players)

For each round, one player is the password-maker, one is the clue-giver, and the others are the guessers. The number of players determines the number of rounds in a game.

The password-maker turns his password over to the clue-giver.

The clue-giver announces the first clue. At this point, any one guesser can call "Me!" and be selected to take a guess. There is no obligation for anyone to take a guess. If a wrong guess is made, that guesser cannot guess again unless every other guesser has taken one guess. After a wrong guess, but before the next clue is given, another player may choose to make a guess.

There are a maximum of five clues given for any password. If a correct guess is made within a five-clue round, the guesser and the clue-giver each score 1 point. If no correct guess is made, the password is revealed and the clue-giver loses 1 point and the password-maker scores 1 point. There is no penalty for a wrong guess.

CATEGORIES

Let your preconceptions scatter to the wind! Contrary to everything the forces of commerce may want you to believe, there's no need to buy an expensive boxful of notecards and a fancy-shmancy 20-sided die to play this classic party game.

SETUP

Each player draws a large 6 x 6 grid of boxes, blacking out the upper left-most box and filling in the other boxes of the top row with five categories agreed upon by the group. The field of possible categories is almost entirely flexible; here are some examples:

Forces of Nature	Jungle Animals
Comic Strips	Building Materials
French Names	Purple Things
Celebrity Criminals	Pro Sports Teams
Things in the Sky	Ugly Actors
Breakfast Foods	Automobiles

Next, five letters are chosen from any magazine, book, menu, or other handy text. The letters are placed in the leftmost column of each player's grid. To ensure a random letter selection, employ one of the following methods:

→ Take the first letter of one line, the second of the next, and so on.

→ Take the seventh to last letter of any five consecutive pages or paragraphs.

→ Close your eyes and lower a pencil point to a text five times.

Every player should now have an identical grid setup.

OBJECT OF THE GAME

To come up with words or phrases that both begin with particular letters and fit into particular categories.

HOW TO PLAY

Time is set at three minutes. Each player tries to fill in her grid with one item beginning with each letter for each category. For example:

	FRUITS	TV SHOWS	WORLD NATIONS	THINGS IN THE OCEAN	LAST NAME OF FAMOUS JOES
B	Banana	Brady Bunch	Botswana	Barnacles	Blow
O	Olive	Oprah	?	Oil Slicks	Olshan
M	Mulberry	McGyver	Madagascar	Marlin	McCarthy
D	Date	Dateline	Denmark	Divers	DiMaggio
V	Vine Peach	Veronica's Closet	Venezuela	Vessels	?

At the end of three minutes, players must stop filling in blanks.

SCORING

Players score themselves by comparing grids and collecting 1 point for every unique legitimate solution to a given blank. In a three-player game, if B: **FRUITS** was filled in with "Banana" by Player 1, "Blueberry" by Player 2, and "Boysenberry" by Player 3, each player would score a point. However, if Player 1 wrote "Banana", Player 2 wrote "Blackberry," and Player 3 wrote "Banana," only Player 2 would score a point.

While creativity is encouraged, players are permitted to contest each others' solutions. The group discusses the matter and votes on whether the solution is legitimate or not. All players get a vote, and majority rules. Ties favor the creator of the contested solution.

→

Here are some examples of contested solutions:

FRUIT

O: **Olive**

Someone might contest, arguing that an olive is a vegetable. The player could knowledgeably refute her, explaining that an olive is a fruit according to the laws of botany.

THINGS IN THE OCEAN

V: **Vessels**

The person who came up with this solution might say, "You know, like a ship! A seagoing vessel." The vote could go either way.

LAST NAMES OF FAMOUS JOES

B: **Blow**

The person who came up with this solution might shrug and say, "Well, I figured I might as well write something." Another player could argue, "But that's not a real person!" A third might chime in, "Still, it's so clever I think we should allow it." Again, it's in the hands of the voters.

LAST NAMES OF FAMOUS JOES

O: **Olshan**

Someone might ask, "Who the heck is that?" The person who came up with it could say, "Joseph Olshan. He wrote *Clara's Heart*. It was made into that Whoopi Goldberg movie." A third player might comment, "Yeah, I've heard of him, but is he really *famous*?" Put it to a vote!

HOW TO WIN

The player with the most points wins the round. Play can continue with scores combined over several rounds to determine an overall winner, or with a threshold score set. ("First to reach 30 points wins the game.")

GRIDWORDS

If you love mind-boggling word games, you've no doubt played a version of this classic on the Internet, or with a boxful of lettered dice at home. As you're about to discover, sometimes it's wonderfully simple to translate a game that millions of people have purchased into a free, more portable format.

SETUP

Each player draws a 4 x 4 grid. A designated round leader makes up a sentence or picks one at random out of a handy book or newspaper, writing it clearly on a piece of paper.

OBJECT OF THE GAME

To form the most valuable words by tracing zigzag paths through a grid of letters made up of the sentence.

HOW TO PLAY

The round leader—who will also keep time—lays the piece of paper with the sentence on the table. In our example, the sentence is **DON'T HAVE A COW, HOMER.** A three-minute time period begins.

Each player writes the first 16 letters of the sentence in the boxes of his grid, from top left to bottom right:

D	O	N	T
H	A	V	E
A	C	O	W
H	O	M	E

Players—including the round leader—then spend the remainder of the

→

round writing a list of all the words of three (or more) letters they can form within the grid.

Words are formed by tracing an imaginary path connecting boxes on the grid; paths can connect any contiguous boxes, moving to the right, to the left, upward, downward, and diagonally.

A few words are highlighted below:

D	O	N	T
H	A	V	E
A	C	O	W
H	O	M	E

CAVE

D	O	N	T
H	A	V	E
A	C	O	W
H	O	M	E

DON (and NOD!)

D	O	N	T
H	A	V	E
A	C	O	W
H	O	M	E

MOOCH

D	O	N	T
H	A	V	E
A	C	O	W
H	O	M	E

COVET

Words cannot use the same letter square twice. For example:

D	O	N	T
H	A	V	E
A	C	O	W
H	O	M	E

MEMO is invalid

Words in the following categories are also invalid:

→ Proper nouns.

→ Words included in the round's generating sentence (**HAVE**, **COW**).

→ Contractions (**DON'T, ISN'T**).

SCORING

When the round leader calls time, all players must stop writing. Each player reads his word list aloud so the others can double-check his words against the grid and against their own lists.

→ Any listed words that cannot be formed on the grid are disqualified.

→ Any words formed by more than one player are struck from all lists.

Players then score their remaining words. Scoring is as follows:

3-LETTER WORDS	1 POINT
4-LETTER WORDS	2 POINTS
5-LETTER WORDS	4 POINTS
6-LETTER WORDS	8 POINTS
7+-LETTER WORDS	16 POINTS

Here's a scored word list from a player in the sample round above:

D	O	N	T
H	A	V	E
A	C	O	W
H	O	M	E

COVE	2	CHAD	2	VENT	2
COO	1	NOD	1	VAN	1
COME	2	DONE	2	VANE	2
CAD	1	CANE	2	VOW	1
HAD	1	CAVE	2	MOW	1
MOVE	2	DOVE	2	MOO	1
HOME	2	OVEN	2	MOOCH	4
COVEN	4	VET	1		
COVET	4	TEN	1		
CHANT	4	NET	1		

51 POINTS

The player with the highest total points wins the round.

→

A full game consists of either a fixed number of rounds (chosen so that each player gets to be round leader an equal number of times) or however many rounds it takes for one player to cross a set point threshold ("200 points wins").

VARIATIONS

→ Enlarge the grid and extend the length of each round.

→ Allow only words with four or more letters.

SAINT MARK'S

 Concocted on a misty Christmas Eve in a Venetian pizzeria near Saint Mark's Square, this pen-and-paper elaboration of Superghost (see page 21) was inspired by Venice's tangle of intersecting alleys that often seem to be going nowhere. Crossword fans and Scrabble® aficionados will be particularly intrigued by this game, which requires intense concentration and mental flexibility. One of its most appealing aspects is the way that, as the competition ends with one player issuing a challenge, the game tends to become a collaborative puzzle that the players work on solving together.

SETUP

Draw a grid of at least 12 x 12 squares. The larger the grid, the longer the game can last.

OBJECT OF THE GAME

To add to an ever-expanding latticework of letters *without* completing any words of three or more letters.

HOW TO PLAY

Player 1 opens the game by writing any letter of the alphabet in any square of the grid. Alternating turns, players fill in one square of the grid with a letter. After the opening move, letters may only be positioned in squares that abut filled squares. There is no limit on the number of times any particular letter may be placed.

Here are the first 12 turns of a sample game. Compare the moves listed with the diagram. Find each placement to get a sense of how the grid begins to evolve. Remember, the placement of a letter must not result in the formation of a complete word.

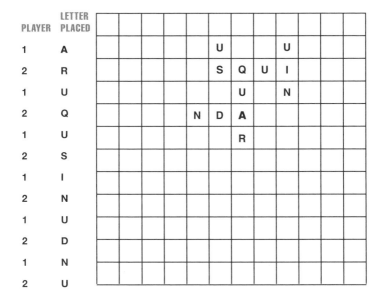

PLAYER	LETTER PLACED
1	A
2	R
1	U
2	Q
1	U
2	S
1	I
2	N
1	U
2	D
1	N
2	U

Play continues until a player is eliminated by accidentally forming a word of three or more letters or until a challenge is issued.

It is essential that players take no notes during the game. Only writing on the shared playing grid is allowed.

CHALLENGES

On any turn, rather than placing a letter, a player can challenge her opponent. The opponent must then demonstrate that *every* horizontal and vertical sequence of two or more letters can be extended to form a word of three or more letters, leaving no meaningless letter sequences in the grid.

If Player 1 issued a challenge at this point, here's one completion strategy Player 2 could propose:

Player 2 has successfully completed the challenge and wins!

If Player 2 failed to meet the challenge, Player 1 would win the game.

Let's return to the sample game, with Player 1 continuing by placing a letter rather than making a challenge.

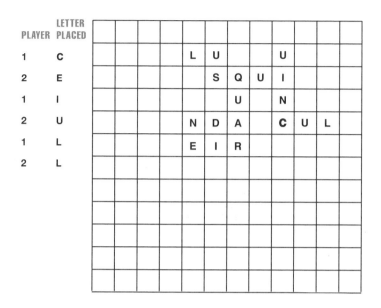

If Player 1 posed a challenge now, Player 2 could fill the grid with the following—except that there is one two-letter sequence (**DI**) left on the grid.

This would not be an acceptable way to complete the board, and Player 1 would win. If Player 2 realized that she was about to leave an incomplete sequence, she could try to extend it by adding on a D to make **DID**, but that would create yet another unworkable two-letter sequence (**DT**). As

→

you can see, things can get complicated quickly. The denser the grid gets, the more difficult it is to place additional letters.

In fact, there are several ways Player 2 could successfully meet the challenge (which also means that there were several placements Player 1 could have made rather than posing the challenge). Here's one:

							Q			
		P	L	U	S		U			
				S	Q	U	I	R	E	
			O		U		N			
	P	A	N	D	A		C	U	L	T
		H	E	I	R		E			
		A		B	E	T				
				S						

HOW TO WIN

The winner of the game is the player who successfully meets a challenge, or the player who makes a challenge that cannot be met.

GRAVILEX

Simple to play yet fiendishly competitive, this word game calls for a strong vocabulary, good spelling ability, and sharp pattern recognition skills. It's played on a six row by seven column Gravity Grid. (To get a feel for how a Gravity Grid works, play The Captain's Mistress on page 54.) With two players, there's lots of opportunity for strategizing; the element of chance is amplified as the number of players increases.

SETUP

Draw a grid of six rows by seven columns.

OBJECT OF THE GAME

To earn the highest score by completing words of three or more letters.

HOW TO PLAY

On each move, a player "drops" any letter of the alphabet into the lowermost empty square of a column. There is no limit on the number of times a given letter may be used over the course of a game.

On alternating moves, a new letter is added to the grid. As early as the third move, words can be formed out of the letters dropped into the grid. A player scores points by identifying and "calling" any words completed by the letter he has dropped into the grid. Words can be formed forward and backward horizontally, vertically, or diagonally.

Here are snapshots from the early stages of a sample two-player game. Player 1's dropped letters are indicated in blue, and Player 2's are in orange.

THIRD MOVE (Round 2)

	C	A	R			

Player 1 drops a C and calls "CAR."

→

FOURTH MOVE (Round 2)

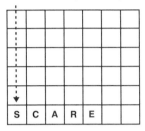

Player 2 drops E and calls "CARE" and "ARE."

FIFTH MOVE (Round 3)

Player 1 drops S and calls "SCARE" and "SCAR."

SIXTH MOVE (Round 3)

Player 2 drops S and calls "SCARES."

SEVENTH MOVE (Round 4)

Player 1 drops O.

EIGHTH MOVE (Round 4)

Player 2 drops B and calls "SOB."

Pay close attention to your own moves. If you overlook a word you've formed, you cannot claim its points later in the game! On the fourth move, above, Player 2 sacrificed a point because he forgot to call the word ERA.

As the grid fills in and letters stack up in columns, words will be formed in eight different orientations. Here are eight models of CAR:

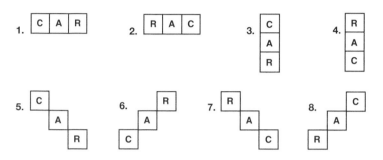

Multiple instances of the same word can be formed and scored during a game.

A game lasts for 42 turns, until the grid is full. The points from each round are then totaled to determine the winner.

SCORING

3-LETTER WORDS	1 POINT
4-LETTER WORDS	2 POINTS
5-LETTER WORDS	4 POINTS
6-LETTER WORDS	8 POINTS
7-LETTER WORDS	16 POINTS

The completed grid below is accompanied by a move-by-move score sheet so you can track the details of a full game.

S	A	S	P	T	I	P
S	B	T	I	N	T	N
N	S	A	S	E	S	O
I	B	H	N	P	B	T
T	A	O	U	I	O	N
S	C	A	R	E	S	T

ROUND-BY-ROUND SCORE SHEET

ROUND #	PLAYER 1		PLAYER 2	
	LETTER DROPPED	WORDS CALLED (pts)	LETTER DROPPED	WORDS CALLED (pts)
1	R	——	A	——
2	C	CAR (1)	E	ARE (1), ERA (1), CARE (2)
3	S	SCAR (2), SCARE (4)	S	SCARES (1)
4	O	——	B	SOB (1)
5	T	REST (2)	U	——
6	N	RUN (1)	I	SIN (1), RIB (1)
7	P	PIE (1), POT (1), TOP (1)	S	SPOT (2), TOPS (2), RUNS (2)
8	A	——	O	CON (1)
9	E	ONE (1), CONE (2)	B	CAB (1), ROB (1)
10	S	ABS (1), CABS (2)	H	HAS (1), HUE (1)
11	N	ION (1)	T	TOE (1)
12	S	SOBS (2)	T	TAO (1), OAT (1)
13	N	PEN (1)	T	PENT (2)
14	I	——	I	ITS (1)
15	N	TIN (1), NIT (1), NITS (2)	S	TINS (2), SNIT (2), SNITS (4)
16	A	BAIT (2)	B	BAN (1), NAB (1)
17	S	ABS (1), NABS (2)	T	HAT (1), TIN (1), NIT (1)
18	S	HATS (2)	T	TEN (1), NET (1), TINT (2)
19	P	PIS (1), SIP (1)	A	ABS (1), ASP (1)
20	I	ITS (1)	O	OBI (1)
21	N	NOT (1), TON (1)	P	PIT (1), TIP (1)
TOTAL SCORE:	39		47	

VARIATIONS

Communal Letter Pool

Instead of allowing each letter of the alphabet to be used an unlimited number of times by each player, letters are withdrawn from a limited pool, created before the game begins. On a blank sheet of paper, write down a full alphabet (26 letters) for as many players as will be participating. If there are three players, the pool will consist of three As, three Bs, etc. If there are only two players, one extra set of vowels should be added, creating a pool of three As, Es, Is, Os, and Us and two of every other letter.

The letter pool is shared by all the players. Only letters in the pool may be dropped into the Gravity Grid. When a letter is placed into the Grid, it is crossed out of the pool.

Personal Letter Pools

Each player gets his own private stash of letters from which to draw. In a two-person game, each player gets one full alphabet, plus one extra set of vowels. If three or more are playing, each gets only a single full alphabet. Each letter in a player's personal pool may only be placed in the Grid one time and must then be crossed out of the pool.

Unique Word Restriction

In this alternative scoring method, points are only earned by a word the first time it is formed during a game. In the sample game above, the word **ABS** was formed—and earned a point—three different times. Under the Unique Word Restriction, only the first player to form the word would have garnered a point.

The Unique Word Restriction can be combined with either of the letter pooling variations.

BONGO

It's a complete coincidence that this game shares its name with a spiral-horned African antelope. But if you're the sort of word lover who would notice that, then welcome! You're going to like it here. This addictive hybrid of Bingo and a wordsearch puzzle is a great way to pass 20 minutes or so. And because it allows for a large number of players, it works as well in a class-room as in a café.

SETUP

Each player draws a grid of 5 x 5 squares.

<table>
<tr><td></td><td></td><td></td><td></td><td></td></tr>
<tr><td></td><td></td><td></td><td></td><td></td></tr>
<tr><td></td><td></td><td></td><td></td><td></td></tr>
<tr><td></td><td></td><td></td><td></td><td></td></tr>
<tr><td></td><td></td><td></td><td></td><td></td></tr>
</table>

OBJECT OF THE GAME

To form as many unique three-, four-, and five-letter words as possible in a 5 x 5 grid. Words can be spelled only forward or backward, horizontally or vertically. Diagonals are not allowed.

HOW TO PLAY

Player 1 chooses any letter of the alphabet and calls it aloud. Without revealing one's grid to the others, each player writes the called letter in any square on his or her grid. Player 2 calls a letter. Each player writes it in any blank square. Play continues until 25 letters have been called, at which point each player's grid is completely full.

There is no limit on the number of times a particular letter can be called. For example, there can be four calls of "E" or five calls of "S" in a game.

As letters are called, players attempt to arrange them in their grids to form three-, four-, and five-letter words along horizontal and vertical axes. Proper nouns and contractions are not allowed.

Words can overlap and can be nested within each other. For example, a player who arranges the called letters **U F S S E** as

F	U	S	E	S

has formed not one, but *four* words: **FUSES, FUSE, USES, USE.**

Words *cannot* be formed diagonally, nor can words turn corners (i.e., all words must lie within a single row or column).

To avoid oversights at the end of the game, players should keep a running list of the words they've formed alongside their grids.

Here are two completed grids based on the same 25 calls along with the wordlists created by the players.

PLAYER 1

B	R	L	N	E
I	O	O	N	S
D	O	O	Z	Y
E	M	U	S	E
T	S	I	L	K

ROOM	KEYS	BIDE	MUSE
MOOR	ILK	BIDET	EMU
ROOMS	SILK	LOO	EMUS
DOOZY	LIST	ZOO	SUM
KEY	BID	MOO	USE

→

PLAYER 2

B	O	D	Y	M
R	O	U	I	S
O	Z	O	N	E
K	E	L	I	T
E	S	L	N	S

BODY	OOZES	LIT	YIN
BOD	OOZE	ZONE	DUO
BROKE	ONE	TIL	
LOUD	OZONE	TILE	
SET	SETS	ORB	

SCORING

Players generate preliminary scores by giving themselves points as follows:

5-LETTER WORDS	10 POINTS
4-LETTER WORDS	5 POINTS
3-LETTER WORDS	1 POINT

In the sample game above, Player 1 would have a preliminary score of 79. Player 2 would have 68.

Players now call their full lists of words aloud. Players are permitted to look at each other's completed grids to verify called words. Once this portion of the game has begun, no one may add words to their lists. Whenever a word is called that appears on more than one player's grid, all players with that word must subtract the point value of the word from their preliminary scores. Once all words have been called and all subtractions have been made, players announce their final scores to determine the winner.

In the sample game above, the two players had no words in common. Their final scores would be the same as their preliminary scores, making Player 1 the winner.

NOTES

→ The fewer players, the more strategy involved; each player has more control of the grid's contents. The more players, the more important it becomes to form uncommon words.

→ It's generally to your advantage to arrange letters so they form words both forward and backward. In preliminary scoring, S P O T S would score a whopping 42 points for SPOTS (10), STOPS (10), SPOT (5), STOP (5), POTS (5), TOPS (5), POT (1), and TOP (1). Of course, the elimination of words duplicated by other players could reduce the point value considerably.

SOLITAIRE CHALLENGES

There's always an element of surprise when more than one player is calling the letters, but you can sharpen your skills with these one-player puzzlers.

The ultimate—and heretofore undiscovered—Bongo letter arrangement would be worth 460 points: 46 points for each row and each column. How close can you get?

How high can you score . . .

→ with no repeated letters?

→ with no letters included more than twice?

→ with only a single vowel of your choice, used as many times as you wish?

INDEX

ACKNOWLEDGMENTS

FIRST MOVE: Bow deeply to Erin Slonaker for being so sharp, engaging, and enthusiastic about her work. I've never had a better editor.

WINNING STRATEGY: Have a couple of free-form brainstorming lunches a year with a gracious, loyal, and ingenious old friend like David Borgenicht and work with a creative designer and illustrator like Susan Van Horn.

I'd like to send wet **X**s and warm **O**s to all my gaming gurus and guinea pigs: Hank and Sheila Gladstone, Walter Smith and Marian McKenzie, Mike McCutchan, Mikey Ciul, Jed Shumsky, Ron Swegman, Ken Gladstone, Tom Grammer, Brian Crane, Murray Scheel, Mike Gaebler, John Cawley, Kelly McQuain, Karen Kudej, Rich Hoglund, Jay Laird, Mattyboy, Jackie Sufak, and Laura Sider, who was literally my right-hand man as I did the final edits with a shattered elbow. I can't wait until my niece and nephews—Leslie, Seth, and Mitchell Gladstone—are old enough to play these games with me and smart enough to beat me at every one of them!

The inspiration for this book drifted in with the mist on a lovely winter's evening in Venice. I'll always be glad that Jeff Abrahamson was there to feel it with me.

THE ANSWERS TO HINKY PINKY PUZZLERS, PAGE 27

HINK PINK	HINKY PINKY	HINKETY PINKETY
Grape ape	Onion bunion	Bahamas pajamas
Star car	Yellow hello	Creation vacation
Rose hose	Liver river	Icicle bicycle

THE ANSWERS TO CODEWORD, PAGE 89

HOPE, LUTE, SLOG